THE PLIGHT OF THE WHALES

THE PLIGHT OF THE WHALES

BY J. J. McCOY

FRANKLIN WATTS
NEW YORK • LONDON • TORONTO • SYDNEY
AN IMPACT BOOK • 1989

Photographs courtesy of: Granger Collection: pp. 13, 35 (bottom), 45, 74; Photo Researchers: p. 16 (Tom McHugh), 50 and 58 (Sam Kimura), 80 (Maurice E. Landre), 86 (Joe Munroe), 135; Culver Pictures: pp. 35 (top), 38; Bettmann Archive: p. 43; UPI/Bettmann Newsphotos: pp. 53, 56, 66, 82, 91, 101, 117; Raymond M. Gilmore: p. 60; Bob Noble/ Marineland of the Pacific Photo: p. 96; NOAA/National Marine Fisheries Service: p. 98; AP/ Wide World: pp. 112, 119, 123, 127; San Diego Convention & Visitors Bureau: p. 130.

Library of Congress Cataloging-in-Publication Data

McCoy, J. J. (Joseph J.), 1917–
The plight of the whales / by J. J. McCoy.
p.   cm.—(An Impact book)
Bibliography: p.
Includes index.
Summary: Discusses how whales have become endangered and the activities of conservation groups.
ISBN 0-531-10778-7
1. Whales—Juvenile literature.   2. Wildlife conservation— Juvenile literature.   [1. Whales.   2. Rare animals.   3. Wildlife conservation.]   I. Title.
QL737.C4M352   1984
639.9'795—dc20   89-5833   CIP   AC

CONTENTS

FOR MY SISTER
THERESA MARIE,
WHO LONG AGO BOUGHT
ME A RECORDING OF
THE CALLS OF THE LOON

PART ONE

THE
WHALES

ONE

The scene is the Pacific Ocean, off the coast of San Diego, California. An excursion boat rocks back and forth on the ocean swells. Lining the rails are men and women with binoculars. They have come not to fish but to observe. Their binoculars focus on what seem to be miniature waterspouts dead ahead. Suddenly, a huge form breaks through the surface of the sea. It is followed by another and still another huge body. There is a loud smacking sound as flukes hit the water.

What the people see are gray whales swimming along the California coast on their annual migration to the breeding grounds in the estuaries and lagoons of Baja California, in Mexico. The whales are the vanguard of a once-numerous species nearly sent into extinction by more than a century of overhunting by American and foreign whalers.

The mention of whales conjures up a number of images to most people. There is the biblical story of Jonah and the whale; Captain Ahab, the mad skipper of the *Pequod*, and his relentless search for the great white sperm whale that bit off one of his legs; and, in more recent times, *Star Trek IV: The Voyage Home*, with its save-the-whales theme. On the darker side, there is the continued slaughter of the ocean leviathans by Japanese, Icelandic, and Norwegian fishermen for "scientific purposes," Faroe Islanders, North Americans, Soviets, and Greenland aborigines. Finally, one might think of the often dramatic and persistent efforts of various environmental and conservation agencies to preserve and protect the dwindling stocks of whales.

Whales have been observed and hunted for centuries by various peoples of the world. The Vikings of Scandinavia and the Basques, a people living along the northern coast of Spain, are regarded as the first whaling societies. Later, Dutch, English, French, and American whaling ships prowled the seas in search of the profitable whales. Yet, despite the hordes of seamen chasing whales and the large number of these great sea mammals that were killed, little was known about the whales. Even Herman Melville, author of the American epic novel *Moby Dick* and a keen observer who spent more than a year aboard a whaling ship, lacked accurate knowledge of the gigantic creatures he and his shipmates saw and captured. The whale, according to Melville and other whalers of the nineteenth century, was simply a huge fish.

Today, of course, we know that whales, like us, are mammals. In fact, we know considerably more about whales than did the whalers and scientists of Melville's day. However, there is still much more to learn if these interesting creatures are to be preserved and wisely managed. Ocean explorers, such as Jacques Cousteau, and marine biologists are constantly adding to the steadily growing dossier on the world's whales, or *Cetacea*.

HERMAN MELVILLE'S *MOBY DICK*, DEPICTED IN 1930 BY
ROCKWELL KENT, WAS A GREAT ALBINO SPERM WHALE.

Whales are completely aquatic mammals, which means that they spend their entire lives in the oceans of the world. Some scientists believe that the ancestors of these giant marine mammals once walked on land. To support this belief, they point to the whale's lungs, warm blood, milk production, vestigial hipbones, and other mammalian features.

If the whales were indeed terrestrial creatures at one time in the earth's history, one may wonder what made them take to the seas. Perhaps, as one theory has it, the ancestors of the whales ventured into the sea in search of sanctuary from the attacks of stronger or more aggressive predators. Or, they may have entered the marine environment in search of a more abundant food supply.

MAMMOTHS OF THE SEA

It is the astonishing size of the larger species of whales that impresses most people. Whales range in size from the small dolphins and porpoises to the great blue whale, the largest creature that ever lived. Blue whales average 90 feet (27 m) in length; some specimens reach 100 feet or more (30 m). The largest blue whale ever recorded was a female that measured 113 feet (33.9 m) from her great head to her flukes. Her weight was estimated at 170 tons.

Whalers and other seafarers know the prodigious strength of the larger whales. Ships' logs—seamen's diaries—and whaling company records contain accounts of the enormous power and strength of blue and sperm whales. One such account records how a female blue whale pulled a 90-foot (27 m), steel-hulled modern whale-chasing boat with its engines running full-speed astern. Despite the reversal of the engines, the whale towed the ship forward at an estimated speed of 5 knots (one knot equals 1.15 miles per hour) for a little more than eight hours. Sticking in the whale's back was a harpoon that weighed more than 300 pounds (135 kg). In addition to this agonizing burden, the whale had to contend with the weight of 2,500 feet (750 m) of 4-inch (10-cm) rope strung out behind her and attached to the whale-chasing boat.

How fast can a whale swim? Estimates vary. It all depends on the species and the individual whale. Some whales have been timed at speeds of 20 knots. Others have traveled faster when swimming in short spurts or dashes. How fast a whale travels when heading straight up to the surface of the sea is a subject for further research. So is the matter of how deep whales dive.

Not all whales dive to great depths. For instance, the baleen whales (see later) have no reason to seek food in the deep-sea valleys. They feed on krill, tiny crustaceans found in the upper layers of the ocean. But the toothed whales, such as the sperm, feed on squid, octopus, and various fish. Consequently, they descend into deep water, where they remain for as long as an hour. When underwater, these whales hold their breath, surfacing at intervals to exhale hot, moisture-laden air from their lungs by way of a blowhole, or spout, on the top of their heads.

Whales are divided into two major groups: the *Mysticeti*, or baleen whales, and the *Odontoceti*, or toothed whales.

BALEEN WHALES

The baleen whales are named for a unique structure in their mouths, a slatlike arrangement of a substance similar in texture to human fingernails. This structure is called *baleen*, or *whalebone*. It grows in long sheets, with a thick fringe on the inner side. The baleen sheets or slats hang down from the upper jaw in a series from back to front. Baleen is tough but flexible; the edges are frayed with long bristles that overlap so that the whale's mouth on each side looks like a hairy doormat.

Baleen acts as a strainer. When a baleen whale finds

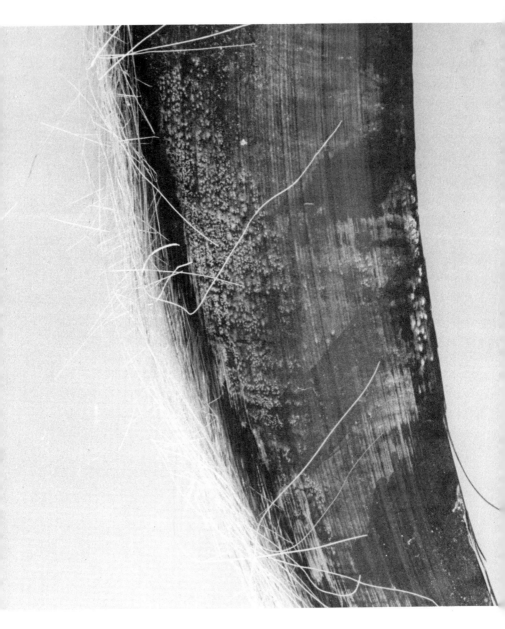

SHEETS OF BALEEN, OR WHALEBONE, HANG
DOWN FROM THE WHALE'S UPPER JAW.

a shoal of krill (also known as *brit*), it swims or plows into the krill, mouth open for scooping in water and krill. The whale then closes its mouth and by raising its huge tongue, squirts out the water and deposits the krill on the baleen slats or plates.

Another feeding method of baleen whales involves holding the mouth ajar, thus allowing water to flow through the gap between the two rows of baleen plates and on out through the side plates, leaving the krill or small fish in the mouth. A third feeding technique consists of thrusting the tongue against the baleen plates to draw water and food into the mouth, then forcing the water out with another action of the tongue.

Northern and Southern Right Whales

The right whales are so-named because nineteenth-century whalers considered them to be the right whales to hunt, for the most profit. Another advantage of the right whale—at least as far as the whalers were concerned—was that it remained afloat after death. Thus, it could be towed to shore or cut up while tied to the side of a ship.

Once there was a large population of right whales roaming the vastness of the North Atlantic, North Pacific, and South Pacific oceans. Each winter, these whales migrated toward the equator. The summers were spent in the far north or south polar regions.

Scientists believe there may be several species of right whales that reach an average length of 50 feet (15 m). The true right whale is black all over its body, but some individuals have white patches on the ventral or underside of their bodies. A unique feature of the right whale is an odd-looking circular area on its snout. This peculiar marking is called the *bonnet*. It is composed of tough, hardened skin that has been invaded by marine worms and other parasites. There is some speculation that this thickened area serves as a bumper similar to that on a car or truck.

Right whales feed by skimming krill from the seawater. The right whales, like most other cetaceans, have a gestation period of a year. This species has been the target of whalers from the twelfth century to the early part of the twentieth century. Unrestricted hunting has exterminated many populations of this species, since females and calves were included as part of the yearly slaughter. Many right whales were killed solely for their baleen, which was used in the manufacture of stays or supports for women's corsets and hoopskirt frames. The right whales are an endangered species and are protected from hunting by international agreement that includes a moratorium on all commercial whaling. The estimated current population of right whales is a few thousand individuals.

Bowhead, or
Greenland, Right Whale
This right whale was discovered by Basque whalers toward the end of the fifteenth century. Eventually, the Basques were joined by Norse, British, and Dutch whalers who relentlessly pursued and slaughtered these whales almost to the point of extinction by the middle of the nineteenth century.

Bowheads average 50 feet (15 m) in length. They have a larger baleen structure than the true right whales; the plates may reach a length of 13 feet (3.9 m) and number over two hundred. The body of the bowhead is thicker in girth than that of the other right whales. Furthermore, the head of the bowhead whale comprises more than a third of its body and has a distinctive bump on top. Bowheads are black in color with white on the chin area and a white band circling the slim tail in front of the flukes.

The bowheads also feed by skimming krill. They are known to breed in late spring in the Davis Strait (the body of water that separates Greenland from Baffin Island) and in the Bering and Chukchi seas (separating Alaska and the Soviet Union). It is believed that the gestation period for the bowhead is one year. Overhunting nearly exterminated the bowhead; their estimated current population is about 8,000. At the present time, the bowheads may only be taken by the Eskimos under a moratorium on whaling decreed by the International Whaling Commission. However, Alaskan, Canadian, and Greenland aborigines are permitted to take a limited number of bowheads for subsistence purposes.

In addition to the right whales, the baleen group includes a subgroup known as *rorquals*. In contrast with the right whales, rorquals sink after death. Thus, they were not the "right" whales for nineteenth-century whalers, although they, too, were hunted until their stocks fell dangerously low. The tendency of the rorquals to sink after death does not pose any problem for modern whalers. Science and technology have overcome that problem. Rorquals can be killed, inflated with air, and towed to shore or hauled aboard factory ships for processing.

Blue Whale
The blue whale is the giant of all whales, averaging 90 feet (27 m) in length. The color is not really blue, but more of a mottled blue-gray above and a lighter gray below. There is a small dorsal fin positioned well back on the body.

Blue whales are found in all the oceans, but because of their great size and food requirements, they are most common in the Arctic and Antarctic regions, where there are vast supplies of krill. Blue whales consume as much as 2 to 4 tons of krill a day; young blues will eat small fish as well as krill. A calf is born every other year or so and is over 20 feet (6 m) long at birth. Calves are weaned at eight months of age.

The blue whale, because of its size and yield of baleen, oil, and blubber, was ruthlessly hunted right up to the 1960s. Once estimated to number more than 100,000, the blue whale stocks have dwindled to about 12,000 individuals scattered in all oceans. Blue whales were placed on the endangered species list by the International Whaling Commission in the 1940s and are included in the current moratorium on commercial whaling. Interestingly, the giant blue whales are sometimes killed by the smaller but predatory killer whales.

Finback Whale

This rorqual is a streamlined whale with a dorsal fin sitting far back on its body. Finbacks, also known as fin whales, grow to an average length of 75 feet (22.5 m). The color is dark gray above and a grayish-white below. Finbacks feed on fish, mainly a herring known as *osmerus*. Finbacks can take in as many as a thousand fish at a time. They also eat krill. They are found worldwide but are less common in tropical waters.

Finbacks are very fast swimmers. They are known to be aggressive and have the ability to charge and even sink a steam-driven whale-chasing boat. After the decline in blue whales, the finback became the leading commercial baleen whale and was heavily hunted until recently. It is now included under the moratorium on commercial whaling. The estimated current population is between 105,000 and 122,000.

Sei, or Sardine, Whale

The sei whale is a fairly common species; however it, too, has been heavily hunted by whalers from many countries. It is named after the seje, or coalfish, because it is often seen off the Norwegian coast when the coalfish arrive there. But the sei does not feed on the coalfish; instead, it feeds on krill in the Atlantic Ocean and on shrimp and sardines in the Pacific Ocean.

Sei whales are dark gray above and whitish-gray below. They reach an average length of 50 feet (15 m). They have an erect dorsal fin located more than one-third of the body length forward from the fluke notch. The seis are great travelers, spending their summers in icy waters and winters in the tropics. Seis can reach a speed of 20 knots when fleeing from a whale-chasing boat. Heavy exploitation has endangered the sei whales, and they are covered by the moratorium on commercial whaling. The estimated current population is 34,000 to 53,000.

Humpback Whale

The humpback whale is one of the better-known whales and is commonly seen by whale watchers on both the Atlantic and Pacific coasts of the United States. The melodious song of the humpback whale—a tuneful olio of sounds that reminds one of a blend of the oboe, cornet, bagpipe, and moog—was first recorded by Dr. Roger S. Payne of the New York Zoological Society's Center for Field Biology and Conservation in the 1950s.

Humpback whales are found in the coastal waters of North America, Europe, Australia, and New Zealand. They reach an average length of 45 feet (13.5 m). The color is black or dark gray above with various amounts of white below. A distinguishing feature of the humpbacks is the large white, winglike flippers, which are used for steering. The humpback is a slow swimmer. When diving, it arches its back, revealing a conspicuous dorsal fin.

Humpback whales feed on krill, squid, and a small fish known as capelin. Capelin, a member of the smelt family, is used as bait for codfish. When the capelin are abundant (May to September off the New England and Newfoundland coasts), humpback whales come to feed on them; consequently, a number of these whales become trapped in codfish nets cast by fishermen after cod that, in turn, are after the capelin. As a result of the net entanglements, humpback whales are not very popular with cod fishermen.

Humpback whales travel in large gams, or schools; they are agile leapers and frolickers, engaging in "talking" and singing. Their numbers have been greatly reduced by overhunting, and they are covered by the moratorium on commercial whaling. The estimated current population is 10,000.

Gray Whale

This whale is also known as the California gray whale. Japanese fishermen know it as *Kou-Kujira*. Coloration consists of various shades of gray, dappled with a dirty-white color. Gray whales lack a dorsal fin. Their main food is a crustacean known as an amphipod, a small marine creature found in seaweed.

There are two populations, or stocks, of gray whales. The California group summers in the northwestern part of the Bering and the Chukchi seas. In late September, this group travels down the west coast of North America to its wintering grounds in the estuaries and lagoons of Mexico's Baja California. The other group, or Korean stock, summers in the Okhotsk Sea and spends its winters in waters off the coast of South Korea, where breeding and calving take place.

The gray whales were heavily hunted in the nineteenth and early part of the twentieth century. Because of the overkill, they disappeared off the coast of California by 1890, after which time they were thought to be extinct. However, the gray whales were rediscovered off the coast of Korea in 1911 by Roy Chapman Andrews, an American naturalist.

Gray whales are aggressive and have been known to attack boats when bull whales were protecting cows or when cows were protecting calves. Gray whales are covered by the moratorium on commercial whaling, and the estimated current number of the two stocks, or groups, is between 16,000 and 18,000.

Minke Whale

The minke is a small baleen whale found worldwide. Its name derives from a Norwegian whaler named Minke, who often confused this small baleen whale with other and larger species. Minke coloration is gray with white on the flippers. This whale attains a length of 25 feet (7.5 m). As the larger baleen whales were protected from commercial whaling, Japanese, Soviet, and other foreign whalers turned to the minke. At present, the minke is protected by the moratorium on all commercial whaling. In 1988, despite the moratorium, Japanese whalers sailed to the Antarctic to capture 300 minke whales for "scientific purposes," an action that was protested by the United States. The current number of minke whales is estimated to be 316,000 to 332,000 worldwide.

Bryde's Whale and the Pygmy Right Whale

These two baleen whales are lesser known. Bryde's whale is a warm-water species often mistaken for the sei. It feeds on krill and small fish that travel in schools, such as sardines and anchovies. It reaches a length of 45 feet (13.5 m). Bryde's whale is covered by the moratorium on commercial whaling.

The pygmy right whale is sometimes mistaken for the minke. However, it has a distinct coloration and profile that helps to distinguish it from the minke and other baleen whales, such as the right and bowhead whales. The size of the pygmy right whale is another field mark; it has an average length of only 16 feet (4.8 m).

TOOTHED WHALES

The toothed whales, or *Odontoceti*, range in size from the freightcar-like sperm whale to the small dolphins and porpoises. Aggressive and predatory, the toothed whales travel the seas in search of squid and fish. Their prey is swallowed whole and digested in the multichambered stomachs of these marine hunters.

Cachelot, or Sperm, Whale

The sperm whale is the largest of the toothed whales, reaching a length of 55 feet (16.5 m). This is the whale that figures in Herman Melville's famous novel *Moby Dick*. (The sperm whale chased by Captain Ahab was an albino sperm whale.) And only a sperm whale could have swallowed Jonah.

The sperm whale was an important keystone in the economic foundation of the New England colonies and later states. It was hunted for its oil and spermaceti, a waxlike substance found in the head of these whales. Sperm oil was used for lighting, while the spermaceti went into the manufacture of candles.

Sperm whales are blackish in color. One-third of the sperm whale's body is composed of its enormous head. This whale has wide, round flippers but no dorsal fin. The sperm whale feeds almost exclusively on squid, and adults may consume as much as 1 ton of squid per day. The sperm whale may dive as deep as 5,000 feet (1,500 m) in search of food and can remain submerged for an hour.

For unknown reasons, a substance called *ambergris* is produced in the intestines of sperm whales. It has been found both during flensing operations and expelled along the shoreline. It has a delightful aroma and is used in the manufacture of expensive perfumes. Sperm whales were relentlessly hunted in the nineteenth century on up to 1988 for their oil and valuable ambergris. They are now protected by the moratorium on whaling.

Baird's Beaked Whale

This whale is second in size to the sperm whale, attaining an average length of 35 feet (10.5 m). Also known as the giant bottlenose, Baird's whale has a bulging fore-head. Found only in the North Pacific, it feeds on fish and squid. It is hunted only around Japan.

Beluga Whale

This whale is also called the white whale. It reaches an average length of 16 feet (4.8 m). Belugas are the source of a superior-quality oil known as porpoise oil, which is used for lubricating scientific and other delicate instruments.

Belugas have an all-white body; they lack a dorsal fin. These white whales are found in the shallow Arctic and Subarctic waters of North America and Eurasia. But they also descend into large northern rivers, such as the Yukon, Churchill, and Saint Lawrence. In severe winters, the belugas have been known to travel as far south as the coastal waters of Japan, Ireland, Scotland, and the Baltic Sea.

Belugas feed on capelin, flounder, halibut, and squid. They are sometimes called *sea canaries* because of their trilling songs, which remind one of the rolling, liquid song of canaries.

In addition to their oil, belugas are hunted for their meat by Inuits (Eskimos) and Aleuts. The estimated current population of beluga whales is 62,000 to 88,000.

Narwhale

This is a northern whale that is rarely seen south of the Canadian and Greenland Arctic regions. The narwhale has a mottled back with a lighter color below. It lacks a dorsal fin.

The distinguishing feature of the narwhale is its long, spiraled horn, or tusk, that grows out from a jaw. This tusk—actually an overgrown tooth—accounts for the whale's nickname of "unicorn of the sea." It is believed that the tusk is used to capture prey, to open holes in the ice, and as a defense weapon.

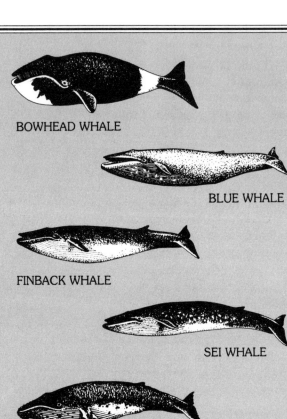

BOWHEAD WHALE

BLUE WHALE

FINBACK WHALE

SEI WHALE

HUMPBACK

GRAY WHALE

MINKE WHALE

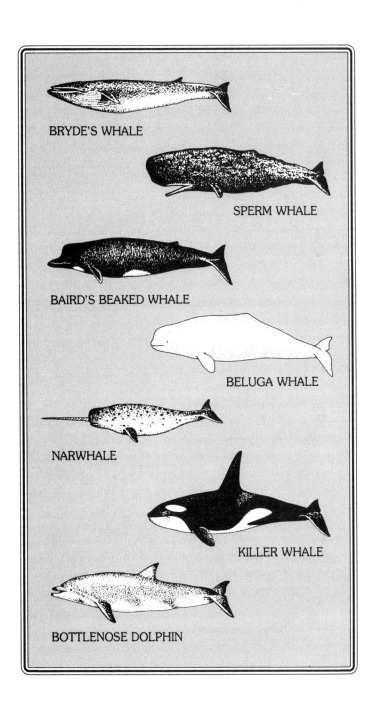

BRYDE'S WHALE

SPERM WHALE

BAIRD'S BEAKED WHALE

BELUGA WHALE

NARWHALE

KILLER WHALE

BOTTLENOSE DOLPHIN

Dolphins and Porpoises

Dolphins and porpoises are small, toothed whales with beaked mouths. Some of them, especially the species seen in films and seaquariums, are familiar to people. Although to the average layperson dolphins and porpoises appear to be similar, there are some important anatomical differences. Porpoises belong to a different family than do the dolphins.

Scientists who have studied and worked with captive dolphins have found them to be alert, intelligent, and cooperative sea mammals that can perform various tasks. The talents and intelligence of dolphins were visually shown in the film *The Day of the Dolphin*, starring George C. Scott.

There are more than twenty-five species of dolphins and six species of porpoises. The largest of the dolphins is the killer whale, or Orca, which reaches an average length of 25 feet (7.5 m). This large dolphin was featured in the motion picture *Orca*, which starred Richard Harris. The killer whale has a shiny black and white body and a prominent dorsal fin. It is found in all waters but is most common in the Arctic and Antarctic regions. Killer whales hunt in packs as large as forty individuals and will attack fish, seals, and, occasionally, even one of the larger whales. However, in captivity the killer whale is gentle with human beings and is kept in sea aquariums for study and display.

Among the dolphins are some smaller species that have come into conflict with people's marine interests, notably the world's fishing industries. Included in this category are the spotted dolphin, Hector's dolphin, the river dolphin, the bottlenose dolphin, the striped dolphin, and the Atlantic white dolphin. In addition to the dolphins, several porpoises have run afoul of fishermen's nets; these are the harbor porpoise, Dall's porpoise, and the spectacled porpoise.

Since dolphins and porpoises often swim close to shore, it is probable they were the first whales to be taken by primitive peoples. These little whales are not too strong and can be captured with light spears from canoes or other small boats. Japanese fishermen can wade out into shallow waters and spear or club porpoises in large numbers.

There is no question that all of the whales, large and small, are beset by problems. Commercial whaling, although banned by a moratorium, continues under what some consider to be the guise of scientific research. Oceanic pollution, with its toxic wastes, nonbiodegradable plastic nets, and other harmful flotsam and jetsam, is an increasing hazard for whales and other marine life. Dolphins, porpoises, and some of the larger whales become entangled in fishing nets and in doing so incur injuries along with the wrath of fishermen. And there is growing concern that whale-watching activities along the whale migratory routes and in the breeding and feeding grounds may even threaten the well-being of the cetaceans. The problems of the whales are not easily solved, for these are international in scope and have economic and political roots, as we shall see in later chapters.

PART TWO

ISSUES AND CONFLICTS

TWO

Although commercial whaling did not reach its peak until the early 1960s, whaling for profit began in the twelfth century with the Basques, who went out in boats off the coast of northern Spain and southern France. In the sixteenth century, the industry grew when an English company, the Muscovy Company, hired Basque whalers to hunt whales. Later, Dutch fishing companies, competitors of the English, engaged Basque whalers to kill whales for them.

Basque whalers hunted black right whales, pursuing them as far as Iceland and Newfoundland. In the sea off Newfoundland, the Basques found another profitable baleen whale—a species later to be known as the Greenland right whale. The remains of a Basque whaling station were unearthed at Red Bay, Labrador, attesting to the great distances traveled by the early Basque whalers.

The Basque whalers were soon joined by fishermen from England, Holland, Denmark, France, Scotland, Sweden, Norway, Iceland, and North America. American whaling—as a commercial venture—started with offshore hunting by Long Island and Nantucket fishermen at the end of the seventeenth century. Eventually, the whaling fever—with its lure of profits from whale oil, spermaceti, and whalebone—soon spread to other New England ports. Salem, New Bedford, Mystic, Gloucester, Marblehead—these Atlantic ports formed the center of the great American whaling industry that sent hundreds of sailing ships to sea in search of the profitable whales.

THE GOLDEN AGE OF WHALING

Whaling in the latter part of the nineteenth century, according to Herman Melville, author of *Moby Dick* and an eyewitness, was a struggle between the largest and strongest mammal on earth and puny man, armed only with a harpoon and a superior brain. Deep-sea whaling was no activity for the timid. Whaling was a very hazardous calling; boatloads of whalers were often hurled into the sea by a frenzied whale, where they drowned or were crushed to death by the gigantic sperm or right whales. Melville wrote this account of a whaling accident:

> *A short rushing sound leaped out of the boat; it was the darted iron of Queequeg [harpooner]. Then all in one welded commotion came an in-*

TOP: THIS 1574 WOODCUT PROVIDES A PICTURE OF THE EARLY FRENCH WHALING INDUSTRY. BOTTOM: WHALING WAS A FIERCE STRUGGLE; BOATLOADS OF WHALERS WERE OFTEN LOST.

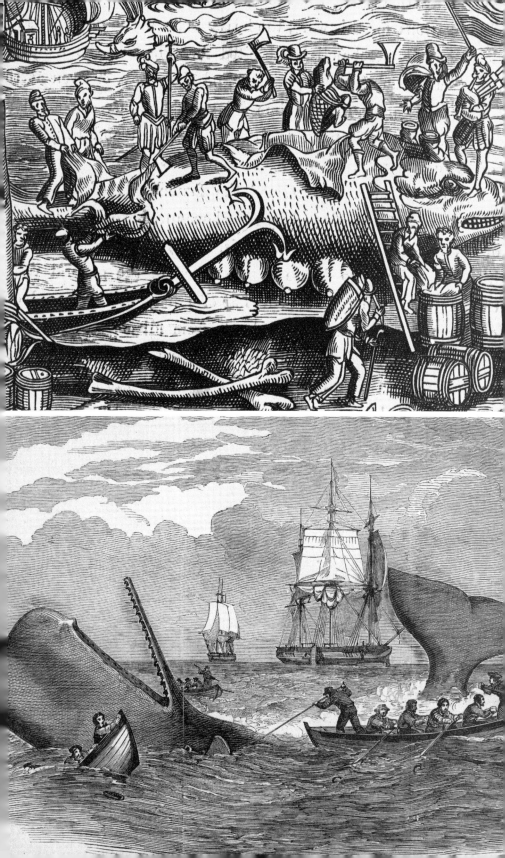

*visible push from astern, while forward the boat
seemed striking on a ledge; the sail collapsed and
exploded. A gush of scalding vapor shot up
nearby; something rolled and tumbled like an
earthquake beneath us. The whole crew were
half-suffocated as they were tossed helter-skelter
into the white curdling cream of the squall.
Squall, whale, and harpoon all blended together,
and the whale, merely grazed by the iron, es-
caped.*

What made nineteenth-century sailors and fishermen
spend from one to five years at sea, risking their lives in
the hot pursuit of whales? Profits for the whaling crew,
from the captain down to the lowly cabin boy. Oil, whalebone, and spermaceti—these products were in great
demand in the nineteenth century. To secure these
products—and hopefully to also enrich themselves—
hundreds of sailors, fishermen, and even farm boys from
the Midwest signed on whaling ships and sailed the seas
in search of the valuable whales.

Lighting the World's Lamps
In the nineteenth century, before the use of gas and petroleum, it was whale oil that lit thousands of streetlights
and home lamps. Whale oil also lit the beacon lamps in
lighthouses on the coasts of North America, lights that
guided ships away from rocks and reefs. Later, whale oil
lit the headlights of locomotives.

Whale Oil as a Lubricant
The spread of the Industrial Revolution, which began in
Europe after 1760, brought an increase in the invention
and production of all kinds of machinery. Sewing machines and other machinery needed to be lubricated to
keep operating at top efficiency. Whale oil suited this

purpose very well, especially sperm whale oil, which can withstand extremes of heat and cold.

At sea, whale oil was poured into barrels (a barrel held about 30 gallons, or 115 liters) and brought back to the New England ports. Some whaling ships that had a run of good hunting returned with as many as 3,000 barrels of the precious whale oil. Just before the Civil War, a gallon of sperm oil was worth $1.75; as the stocks of sperm whales decreased, the price rose to $2.00 a gallon, a good price in those days.

Whalebone

The value of baleen, or whalebone, like oil and whale meat, varied with the supply, demand, and competition from substitutes. In general, the price of whalebone (averaging about $1.50 after the Civil War) increased as more uses for it were found. A strong, springy, hard substance, whalebone was taken mainly from the right whales, bowheads, humpbacks, and California gray whales. Although a main component of women's corsets, whalebone was also used in the manufacture of horsewhips. When whalebone became too expensive to use in making horsewhips, rawhide was used as a substitute. Other popular uses of whalebone included umbrella ribs, stiff-bristle brushes, chair and sofa springs, and for the manufacture of certain fine or delicate instruments.

Ambergris

A prize whale byproduct—rare though it was (and is) and sought by whalers from many world ports—was ambergris. This substance is found in the intestines of sperm whales. While ambergris was usually taken from the whale, it was sometimes found floating on the surface of the sea or on coastlines. Some chunks of ambergris weigh as much as 200 pounds (90 kg).

Ambergris is gray in color and has the texture of grainy cheese or cork. What is remarkable about am-

bergris is that it gives off a most pleasant odor. In some countries, ambergris was used as a medicine and spice. But its chief value in the nineteenth century was its ability to fix or stabilize volatile oils from which rich perfumes were made. What ambergris does is to preserve the fragrance of perfumes for long periods of time. It does this by absorbing other, unwanted odors.

Nineteenth-century whalers were on the lookout for sperm whales that might yield the precious ambergris. A whale with ambergris meant a lot of money for the crew and shipowner or company. In what has been called the Golden Age of Whaling, ambergris was worth more than a whole shipload of baleen and oil. Only a few whaling ships were lucky enough to find ambergris. The largest yield of ambergris taken from one whale, by a New England whaler, weighed more than 900 pounds (410 kg).

Whale Meat

Whale meat, or whale beef, as it was also called, was historically an important staple in the diet of the Japanese, although local settlements elsewhere have also depended on it. Whale meat resembles beef in texture and color. Belly meat was often called whale bacon. While whale meat did not bring the high prices that oil, baleen, and ambergris did, it was another valued product from the whales.

THE WHALE HUNTERS

Nineteenth-century whalers were a rough, often cruel, and quarrelsome lot of men. The nature of their work,

WHALEBONE—STACKED IN BUNDLES FOR FACTORY PROCESSING—WAS USED FOR CORSETS, UMBRELLAS, HORSEWHIPS, AND OTHER PRODUCTS.

especially its brutality, could eventually turn even the most easygoing person into a hardened, callous, and unfeeling individual. Life aboard the average whaling ship was no seagoing vacation or cruise. It was usually a tedious and often boring and isolated existence, with men forced to live in cramped and close quarters. Personality conflicts, petty quarrels, and real or fancied wrongs often erupted into violence and even killings. The logs of many whaling ships recorded upheavals among their crews and officers.

Although the Golden Age of Whaling provided big profits for shipowners and companies, it did not provide crews with much in the way of diversion or recreation. Nineteenth-century seamen, unlike those of today, did not have much to do in the way of amusement. They did not have radios, television, or electronic games. There were few books on board most whaling ships; many crewmembers could not read or write. Literate seamen, such as Herman Melville and Charles Dana (both of whom eventually wrote books about their sea experiences), were among the lucky few who could while away their idle hours by reading.

Long months at sea, away from home and family and familiar things, produced some gloomy times for the whalers. Homesickness, especially among the younger seamen, was a common ailment. Those seamen who could write did put down their thoughts of the sea and the home life they missed so badly:

> *O how I wish I was at home today—to go to meeting, and tonight to see the girls. That's what I like is the girls—girls forever for me, I say! So ends the day, but homesick.*
> *(From a whaler's journal, 1852*
> *New Bedford Whaling Museum)*

However, there was one popular form of diversion for nineteenth-century whalers. It was engaging in what they called a "gam." When another ship came within hailing distance, the crews would line the rails and call out to each other. And when the ships moved closer and lay side by side, the seamen on both ships—starved for news or sight of a new face—visited back and forth on the ships. They gossiped and told stories of their adventures at sea. Many of them exchanged gifts, usually things made out of cord and rope, a kind of sailor's macrame. Others gave each other elaborately carved scrimshaw, objects carved on and from whalebone or teeth.

Herman Melville—and he was one of the premiere historians of nineteenth-century whaling—did not have a high opinion of whaling crews. Nor did he think much of conditions aboard the whaling ship on which he served. Although he was at first excited by the promise of adventure and travel aboard the *Acushnet*, a whaling ship out of New Bedford, Melville became disillusioned by the reality of life at sea. He was disgusted and fed up with the quarrelsome crew of the *Acushnet*. After a year, he jumped ship when the vessel was off the Marquesas Islands in the South Pacific.

Melville was not alone in this disillusionment; other seamen, particularly those from the Midwest farms, found life aboard a whaler far from what they expected. There was no harmony or discipline aboard the average whaling ship, nor was there much attempt at keeping the ships taut and tidy. In a sense, it was a hopeless task to keep a whaling ship clean. The very nature of the gory business—with its slippery oil, blood, guts, decaying meat, and the powerful, lingering, penetrating stench that infiltrated every part of a ship—turned a sailing ship into a vessel of carnage and filth. Merchant and naval seamen claimed they could smell a whaling ship miles away when the whaler was to the windward.

Yet, despite the appalling conditions aboard the nineteenth-century whalers, men signed on for the long voyages. When they did sign the ship's articles, they did so for the duration of the voyage, which could range from one to five years. The standard pay agreement—called a *lay*—was a certain share of the profits made from the whale products. These shares were prorated according to rank.

This sharing of profits (or losses) helped the whaling crews to endure the harsh and bloody life aboard the whaling ships. The sharing plan also aided shipowners, for they often had trouble signing on a full crew. Few seamen wanted to sail on a whaler; merchant seamen scorned service aboard whaling ships, and owners were forced to accept whoever agreed to sign the articles. Consequently, many a whaling ship's crew was made up of adventurers, misfits, and even criminals.

PRESSURE ON THE WHALES

The profits for the shipowners and the shares for the crews put great pressure on the stocks of whales. There was no thought of managing the whale stocks. It was simply a matter of the more whales killed on a voyage, the greater the profits for all hands. Few people knew anything about species numbers, population dynamics, reproduction rates, or migration habits and routes. Melville devoted a chapter to his ideas on the natural history of the whale. The chapter contains passage after passage of detailed descriptions of whales—their physical makeup and habits observed from aboard a whaler. But Melville was no marine biologist or zoologist; he, like most people of the time, thought the whale was simply a large fish.

THE WHALERS' WEAPONS
WERE HARPOONS.

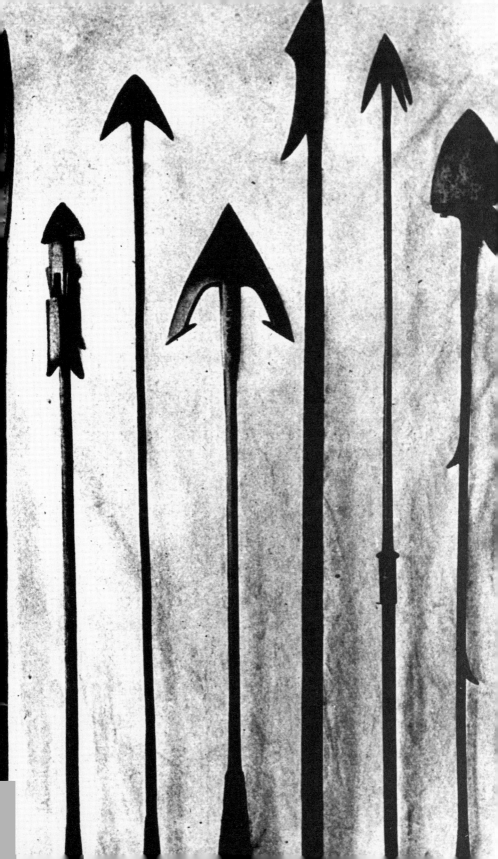

Here is a passage from Melville's chapter on cetology:

Be it known that, waiving all argument, I take the good old fashioned ground that the whale is a fish, and call upon holy Jonah to back me. This fundamental thing settled, the next point is, in what internal respect does the whale differ from other fish? In brief, they are these: lungs and warm blood; whereas all other fish are lungless and cold blooded . . . to be short, then, a whale is a spouting fish with a horizontal tail.

Mention should be made of the types of ships used in the nineteenth century for whaling. They were usually brigs, schooners, barks, or full-rigged ships.

Brig
The brig, or brigantine, was a two-masted square-rigged vessel. There were three classes of brigs, depending on the rigging. The main mast had a standing gaff or spar that was equipped with a small fore-and-aft sail of a triangular shape.

Bark
The bark, or barque, was a three-masted vessel with the foremast and mainmast square-rigged, while the mizzenmast was fore-and-aft rigged. The fore-and-aft sail could be hoisted or lowered.

Schooner
The schooner was the most popular whaling vessel used during the nineteenth century. It is believed to have originated in New England. The term *schooner* derives from an older word, *scoon*, which meant "to skim over the water."

Schooners are fore-and-aft rigged vessels with two or more masts. Three- and four-masted schooners ap-

A NINETEENTH-CENTURY FLEET OF WHALING
SHIPS WAS AN IMPRESSIVE SIGHT.

peared in 1840; by the 1880s, five- and six-masted schooners weighing 2,000 to 3,000 tons were built. The New England fishing and whaling fleets of the latter nineteenth century employed these graceful, speedy vessels until their replacement by steam-powered ships in the twentieth century.

Other Ships

Very large sailing ships were also used for whaling; they were usually full-rigged vessels with large, square sails and three masts. These big ships required crews of up to forty seamen. Old merchant ships were sometimes converted into whalers, especially if they had large holds in which many barrels of the precious whale oil could be stored.

Each whaling ship had a number of whale boats—strong, heavy-planked boats that carried the harpooner and oarsmen as they chased a whale. Built of stout oak and constructed to withstand rough, heavy seas and the battering by high winds, the whale boat was a crucial factor in the capture of a whale. It was from the prow of a tossing whale boat that the harpooner heaved his heavy harpoon or iron into a fleeing sperm or right whale. An average whale boat had a crew of six seamen, but could hold twelve men.

AN ERA OF
PROFIT AND LOSS

The Golden Age of Whaling was a time of big profits for many shipowners and companies. However, the discovery of rock oil out near the Allegheny River in western Pennsylvania after the Civil War brought a decline in the demand for whale oil, a decline that increased rapidly as oil wells began to appear throughout Pennsylvania and the American Southwest.

Although the price of whale products decreased in the late nineteenth century, more than a dozen nations continued to send fleets out after the baleen and toothed whales. There was little letup in the hunting of the sea leviathans. They were a natural resource for the taking, a source of raw material that could be turned into profits.

INTO THE
TWENTIETH CENTURY

The relentless exploitation and slaughter of the whales spilled over into the twentieth century, despite a big decline in the demand for and price of whale products. No one knew how many whales were left in the seas. No one thought about managing this dwindling natural resource. Then, after tens of thousands of blue whales had been killed in the 1930s, whalers began to have difficulty finding any of these giants of the sea. A few nations, notably the United States, were beginning to become concerned about the decimation of whale stocks; they wondered just how long the killing could go on.

Motivated by the United States, several nations endorsed some international measures for reducing the pressure on the beleaguered blue whale. However, the recommended measures met with strong opposition from Japan and Germany and were never effective. Nothing was done about conserving the dwindling stocks of blue whales, and this species went into a steep dive toward extinction. It was not until the defeat of Japan and Germany in World War II that any hope of preserving and managing the blue whale population arose.

Whaling had virtually ceased during the war, as whaling vessels were used in combat support roles. As the war ended, concerns arose over the uncontrolled resumption of whaling, particularly in the Antarctic, and the implications this would have for the global whale oil market.

THREE

When the blue whale stocks went into a sharp decline, commercial whalers turned to the hunting of finback whales in the Antarctic. The familiar pattern of concentrating on the most profitable species was repeated. Whaling became the greatest of all big-game hunting, and whalers from a dozen nations went after the fin whales. Whenever a rare blue whale was sighted, it, too, was taken, along with any right, sei, or gray whales that came within view of the twentieth-century whalers.

What should have been expected, especially since the blue whale was a prime example, happened. The stocks of finback whales began in the 1960s to show signs of population decrease.

INTERNATIONAL
WHALING CONVENTION

A number of whaling nations sent delegates to the International Whaling Convention held in Washington, D.C., in 1946. The delegates discussed the decrease in baleen whale stocks and possible measures for controlling whaling and catch quotas. There were many arguments and disagreements as to what should be done about managing whale stocks and whaling. However, an important development of the conference was the creation of the International Whaling Commission, or the IWC as it is commonly called.

The main function of the IWC is to review and revise as necessary the following whale-protection measures:

1. Provide complete protection for certain species or stocks of whales.
2. Designate specific ocean areas as whale sanctuaries.
3. Set maximum catch limits on whales taken in any one whaling season.
4. Prescribe open and closed seasons and areas for commercial whaling.
5. Fix size limits above and below which certain species may not be killed.
6. Prohibit the capture of suckling calves and females with calves.
7. Require regular reports on catches and other statistical and biological data; each member nation's whaling fleet is required to turn these reports in to the IWC.

The IWC also encourages, coordinates, and, to a limited extent, funds research on whales and promotes studies into related matters, for example, the humaneness of certain whale-killing methods. Another important function of the IWC is to regulate and manage the killing of whales by aborigines.

Membership in the IWC is open to any nation that agrees to abide by the rules and schedules laid down at the 1946 international conference or that have been established by the commission. Each member country is represented on the IWC by a commissioner, who has a

staff of scientists and advisers. The commission chairperson and vice-chairperson are elected from among the commissioners, and each serves for a period of three years. The IWC headquarters are located in Cambridge, England. Meetings are held annually, usually in June, and may convene in any member nation.

LACK OF SCIENTIFIC
DATA ON WHALES

The creation and organization of the International Whaling Commission was an important step toward preserving whale stocks and controlling whaling operations. But in its early days, the IWC was operating in the dark; little was known about the habits, migration routes, and populations of the commercial whale species. All kinds of questions and problems arose regarding control measures. For example, were the blue whales actually in a population decline? If so, how much of a decline? And were the other commercial species—fin, sei, right, and gray whales—also in trouble, as some nations alleged? These and other questions had to be resolved before any intelligent and effective protection program could be put into force by the IWC.

INCREASE IN WHALING

Although the demand for whale products decreased after World War II, mainly because substitutes became available, whaling operations actually increased. Whale-chasing boats and factory ships from a half-dozen nations combed the Antarctic seas for whale stocks. Even the

WHALES HAVE BEEN AN
IMPORTANT FOOD SOURCE.

drop in the number of whales sighted did not make Japan, the Soviet Union, Norway, the Netherlands, and the United Kingdom—the chief whaling nations—cut back their operations. Japan's wartime devastation brought an increased demand for whale meat, a prized source of protein for the Japanese people. Much to the dismay of the United States, Japanese whalers continued to hunt and kill whatever whales came their way.

Japanese scientists and fisheries officials sought justification for their intense whaling operations. Dr. Masaharu Nishiwaki, a professor at the Ocean Research Institute, University of Tokyo at Nakano, Japan, defended Japan's killing of whales for meat and other products. "People in the world have widely diverse tastes and religious restrictions in their choice of foods," stated Nishiwaki. "We must have thoughtfulness for such differences of diverse peoples of the world."

In the 1950s, the Soviet Union increased its whaling operations despite signs of diminishing whale stocks. The Soviets launched a long-range plan to build more modern whaling fleets. They increased their Antarctic fleets to four, which included two of the largest whale-factory ships ever built. But even the Soviet Union, as well as Japan, had to face facts. If the intense hunting of whales continued, eventually there would not be enough whales to go around or to support such a concentrated and technological industry as whaling had become in the second half of the twentieth century.

A CALL FOR MORE SCIENTIFIC DATA ON WHALES

The IWC had not been very effective in protecting the endangered whale stocks. Commissioners did not act on the recommendations of their scientific advisers. There was no question that the IWC and its member nations needed more information about the whales and their pop-

A WHALE IS CUT UP ON THE DECK
OF A SOVIET WHALING SHIP.

ulations. After considerable urging by the United States and a few other concerned nations, the IWC finally agreed to hire a small group of experts in the field of population dynamics. The mission of these experts was to study the entire problem of the whales in the Antarctic region, the main hunting grounds. The experts, known as the Committee of Three, were instructed to assess the stocks of all baleen whales, estimate the sustainable yield of each species, and, from their findings, make recommendations as to the allowable catch for each species.

A FORMIDABLE TASK FOR THE COMMITTEE OF THREE

The Committee of Three faced a difficult task. The blue whales were in the most dangerous position. The experts had to arrive quickly at a workable estimate of the blue whale stocks. They had to do the same for the sei, fin, sperm, right, and gray whales. They had to determine the rate of natural mortality for the various groups of whales. The three experts and their staffs also had to amass data on the changes in catches of whales. The frequency of sightings of the different species was another important part of the research. Finally, each whaling company would have to provide information on every whale killed in the past ten years.

The Committee of Three issued a preliminary report in 1963. What came out of all the research was the dismal fact that the Antarctic stocks of whales, particularly fin whales, were in jeopardy. Increased pressure on these whales—uncontrolled hunting—could send them into complete extinction. Despite this discouraging news, little agreement was reached by the whaling nations on catch quotas, whaling techniques, and conservation measures. The perilous situation of the whales remained as it had been.

MODERN WHALING

Whaling today is far different from what it was in the days of Herman Melville and the Golden Age of Whaling. Whale hunting in the Antarctic region—the "happy hunting grounds" of modern whalers—is a highly complex and technological industry. Whalers no longer spend several years at sea chasing whales. Nor do seamen launch sturdy whale boats and furiously row after fleeing whales. Whaling is generally limited to six or seven months a year, according to IWC regulations. Instead of the man-powered whale boats, whales are chased by power boats known as *catchers*. And the heavy, sharp-pointed, hand-held harpoons or irons shot into whales by nineteenth-century harpooners are relics of a bygone time, seen now only in whaling museums. The modern harpoon, invented by a Norwegian whaler, Sven Foynd, weighs several hundred pounds and has an explosive head. It is fired from a cannon on the bow of the catcher boat.

Factory Ships
Gone are the sail-rigged barks, brigs, schooners, and whale ships that plied the seas in the nineteenth century. In their place are giant seagoing factory ships capable of processing whales in a relatively short time. The factory ship crew is composed of regular seamen and factory workers, similar to slaughterhouse workers on shore. These floating factories are compact, highly efficient units that cater to as many as 400 people who live aboard. The ships contain living quarters, a dining room, a theater, a hospital, laboratories, and recreational and other facilities necessary to ensure a successful whaling season. Factory ships cost about $20 million.

Catcher Boats
The catcher boats range in weight from 350 to 700 tons, depending on the type. Some are converted World War

MODERN WHALERS USE POWERFUL HARPOON GUNS.

II Corvettes. Catcher boats are fast and maneuverable boats that average 20 knots an hour. Fifty-five or ninety millimeter cannons mounted high in the bows fire the iron explosive-laden harpoons that are set to go off moments after penetrating a whale's body. One shot is intended to kill a large whale, such as a blue, in about fifteen minutes. However, poor marksmanship or faulty explosives may require several shots to be fired into a hapless whale.

Catcher Boat Crews

Whale-chasing crews have not changed much since the Golden Age of Whaling. Catcher boat crews are composed of hardy, rugged, and sometimes callous seamen and hunters. The duty of the catcher boat is to locate, kill, and tow whales to the factory ship. In some whaling fleets, a special towing boat is used, thus freeing the catcher boats to go after more whales.

When the whales are brought to the factory ship (they have usually been injected with pressurized air to keep them afloat), the carcasses are hauled onto a deck. This is done by dragging the whales up a ramp located in the stern of the factory ship. Once up the ramp, the whale is moved forward by means of a conveyor mechanism and dismembered in stages by the factory workers.

The first stage in whale processing takes place at the top of the stern ramp. Here, flensers—workers armed with sharp long-handled knives or special flensing tools—strip the blubber from the whale carcass. The blubber strips are dropped into large holes in the deck that lead down to the cutting or dicing machines that chop the blubber into small chunks.

After the cutting or dicing, workers place the blubber into high-pressure cookers to separate the valuable oil. As the oil moves along the assembly line, it is purified, or refined. All water is removed, and the oil is stored in huge tanks located in the factory ship's hold.

Next, the whale carcass, minus the blubber, is

A FLENSER STRIPS THE BLUBBER
FROM A WHALE CARCASS.

dragged forward to another station, where workers remove the meat. When all of the meat has been removed, the carcass is again hauled forward to a point where the bones are removed and sawed up. The whale's entrails and other unusable portions are heaved overboard for sharks and other fish to fight over and eat. All in all, whale processing is a bloody affair.

All Is Not Easy Sailing

Whaling today is not without problems. The decline in whale stocks is a major concern, and the success of any whaling fleet now depends on a mixture of luck and skill. If too many fleets try to hunt whales in the same region, there is bound to be a shortage of whales for some of those fleets. The situation is similar to that of a stream or river packed with fishermen, all trying to catch the few fish there. For the whalers, the situation is compounded when hordes of catcher boats steam around, scattering and alarming the whales.

Despite modern technology, whalers still face some forces of nature beyond their control. High winds can break up or disperse the water from a whale's spout. When this occurs, whalers have difficulty in sighting a whale, because only a small portion of a whale's body is out of water. Thus, the spouting water is an important indicator of the presence of a whale.

Then there are the heavy seas and storms that can make whaling not only difficult but hazardous. Harpooning and towing whales are slow and laborious tasks. Furthermore, the big factory ships roll in heavy seas, which makes the dismembering of the whale carcass a difficult and often hazardous process. Usually, in stormy weather and high seas, whaling operations cease.

However, the problems and risks of whaling were and are an accepted part of the industry. In spite of them, more than 2 million whales have been slaughtered in this century and turned into lubricants, pet food, shoe polish,

SPOUTING WATER ALERTS WHALERS TO
THE PRESENCE OF A WHALE.

paint, soap, margarine, fertilizer, car wax, lamp oil, machine oil, and human food.

Terrestrial wildlife managers have learned that no species can stand continued decimation without efforts or programs to stabilize their populations. This is as true for whales as it is for deer, waterfowl, and other game species. Marine biologists know that if whale stocks are to survive, their population dynamics must be understood and overhunting must be prevented. Whales must be wisely managed if they are to remain a viable natural resource. Annual catches of whales must be geared to what is known as the maximum sustainable yield. What this means is that only those whales should be taken that can be killed without endangering the ability of the species to sustain and reproduce itself. Up to the present moratorium on whaling, this principle was not applied to whales.

True, the maximum yield principle when applied to the harvesting of whales will permit only moderate catches of endangered or threatened species. The blue, sei, sperm, bowhead, right, and humpback whales can stand only so much hunting. The major whaling nations, such as Japan and the Soviet Union, will have to be content with smaller catches if the moratorium ends and commercial whaling resumes. But by following the sustainable yield rule, whaling nations would be ensured of a permanent supply of whales.

FOUR

In December 1971, the last U.S. whaling station, located in California, closed its doors. The Del Monte Fishing Company—a relic of the great American whaling industry that once sent more than 700 ships out to sea in pursuit of the profitable whales—also ended its whaling activities in the same year with a catch of a hundred whales. The United States, once the greatest of whaling nations, became the leader in a campaign to save the whales.

The U.S. decision to stop whaling activities followed a plea made by Under Secretary of State U. Alexis Johnson at a meeting of the International Whaling Commission in Washington, D.C., in June 1971. Johnson pleaded with the IWC to act to save the world's diminishing stocks of whales. After Johnson's plea, Congress passed a joint resolution directing the U.S. Department of the Interior to seek a worldwide ten-year moratorium on commercial whaling. Some nations were receptive to the recommendation, others were not. The chief whaling nations that opposed the moratorium were the Soviet Union and Japan, nations with whaling fleets that accounted for 85 percent of the world's whale catches.

ENDANGERED WHALE LIST

The Interior Department placed eight whale species on its endangered species list. These were the blue, sei, sperm, right, gray, bowhead, fin, and humpback whales. As a result of the endangered species classification, the department banned the importation of all products made from these whales, including oil, spermaceti, meat, teeth, bone, ambergris, and scrimshaw (carvings on whalebone and teeth). And the United States called on all whaling nations to cease their whaling operations.

UN CONFERENCE ON
THE HUMAN ENVIRONMENT

The subject of whaling was on the agenda of the UN Conference on the Human Environment held in Stockholm, Sweden, in 1972. Delegates to the conference expressed concern for the survival of the world's whale stocks. The call by the United States for a ten-year moratorium on whaling was put into a resolution, with twelve nations abstaining. The final vote for the resolution was 53–0.

MORATORIUM DEFEATED
AT IWC MEETING

When the International Whaling Commission met in July 1972, tough opposition to the moratorium came from Japan and the Soviet Union. Subsequent meetings did produce some significant achievements. U.S. negotiators managed to obtain a reduction in the number of whales that could be legally harvested in the Antarctic and the North Pacific regions, areas where the fleets of Japan and the Soviet Union took the largest share of whales. However, the overall result of the IWC meetings was one of managing the whales for oil and meat, rather than for ensuring their survival. Many people in the United States—government officials as well as ordinary citizens— were disappointed over the failure to obtain a total moratorium on whale killing.

Congressman John D. Dingell (Michigan) lauded the efforts of the delegates to the UN Conference on the Human Environment for their support of the American recommendation for a ten-year moratorium. "On an international level, however, these responsible efforts have apparently been in vain. Though the International Whaling Commission has strongly urged management principles to conserve the stocks of great whales, the Governments of Japan and Russia have consistently rebuffed these efforts and apparently have no intention of slowing down. . . . so, over the objections of the United States and other concerned whaling and non-whaling countries, the USSR and Japan are proceeding with their race for the last great whales."

WHALING OBSERVER PLAN

IWC commissioners, with some exceptions, agreed to what was known as the Whaling Observer Scheme. Under this plan, international observers would be allowed to board whaling ships to inspect catch quotas and the species taken. As was expected, the Soviet Union strenuously objected to having outside observers on board their factory ships. Ultimately, the Japanese and Soviet whalers, however, did agree to the plan in 1972.

The wrangling over whale protection, catch quotas, and hunting regions continued into the 1980s. Norway, Japan, Peru, and the Soviet Union initially refused to sanction a moratorium on commercial whaling. All have since abided by it in strict terms, although, as noted earlier, some whaling for scientific purposes continues.

THE MORATORIUM BECOMES INTERNATIONAL LAW

In 1982, ten years after the proposal by the United States, the International Whaling Commission decided by a vote of 25 ayes, 7 nays, and 5 abstentions to prohibit commercial whaling indefinitely. The resolution stated that "catch limits for the killing of commercial purposes of whales from all stocks for the 1986 coastal and the 1985/86 pelagic [open seas] seasons and thereafter shall be zero."

The resolution went on to state that the moratorium would be subject to review, based on the best scientific advice. By 1990 at the latest, the commission would undertake a comprehensive assessment of the effects of the moratorium on the whale stocks. Furthermore, the commission, based on the assessment, would consider modification of the resolution and the establishment of other catch limits.

Four whaling nations—Norway, Peru, Japan, and the Soviet Union—filed formal objections to the moratorium. Under regulations of the 1946 whaling convention held in the United States, all member countries are entitled to make such objections, and once the objections are filed, none of the objecting nations is bound by the moratorium. This loophole and another—"whaling for scientific purposes"—was to prove a problem in the late 1980s.

MORE WHALES ON PROTECTED LIST

Over a three-year period (1985–88), the International Whaling Commission extended protection to four more

A SOVIET WHALING FLOTILLA
TOWS ITS CATCH TO PORT.

stocks of whales. These included three groups of minke whales and one of Bryde's whales; all of these stocks are found in the Northern Hemisphere. Also in this period, Japan and the Soviet Union hunted minke whales in the Antarctic seas under their objection rights. Norway's minke whale killing continued under the objection procedure, and Japan's coastal whaling operations for sperm, minke, and Bryde's whales continued under the objection procedure in the summers of 1986 and 1987.

Under IWC regulations, whaling operations carried out under objection are not restricted as to the number of whales that can be taken. However, all of the objecting nations have indicated that they would adhere to self-imposed catch limits on the advice of the IWC's Scientific Committee. Any commercial whaling that continues is still subject to all other regulations, for example, the regions in which whaling may be done, the length of the whaling season, the species taken, the size of whales taken, and the variety of species taken in a whaling season.

PACKWOOD-MAGNUSON AMENDMENT

In 1984, the Reagan administration entered into a bilateral agreement with Japan that allowed Japanese whalers to continue killing whales for two years after the IWC moratorium was to go into effect. During this period, the United States would not impose any economic sanctions on Japan if that nation agreed to abide by other IWC rules. More than ten environmental and animal welfare groups challenged this agreement, arguing that Japan should cease all whaling after the moratorium went into effect. Lawsuits were filed by these organizations. However, the U.S. Supreme Court ruled 5–4 to uphold the Reagan administration's agreement with Japan. The reasoning was that the agreement was a step forward in getting the Japanese to eventually cease their whaling operations.

Two years later, the Japanese government announced a phased and conditional withdrawal of its objection to the moratorium on commercial whaling. For example, Japan insisted that its fleets be allowed to continue open-sea hunting of minke whales, coastal taking of minke and Bryde's whales, and coastal hunting of sperm whales in the 1987 whaling season. The Japanese said, however, that if the United States imposes any trade sanctions against Japan at any time during the phasing out of whaling operations, Japan will resume whaling. It would do so under the objection procedure of the IWC.

THE SOVIET UNION
CEASES WHALING

The Soviet Union announced to the IWC that it planned to prohibit whaling in the 1988 season because of "technical reasons." What these technical reasons were has never been stated. The Soviet delegate to the IWC reported that such a halt in whaling operations was only temporary. However, when the Soviet Union resumed whaling (under its right as per the IWC objection procedure), it would be in accordance with the IWC Scientific Committee recommendations.

WHALING FOR
SCIENTIFIC PURPOSES

In 1986, the governments of Iceland and the Republic of Korea issued permits to fishing fleets to continue whaling as part of their scientific research programs. Such whaling was allowed under the IWC regulations formulated in 1946. The Republic of Korea's scientific program was to last for one season.

Iceland's proposal was to be part of a wide-ranging, long-term research program that included whale stock surveys and radio-tagging of whales. Iceland's project, based at the International Research Center in Iceland, allows for the participation of scientists from other countries. This scientific project is funded by proceeds from whaling operations; that is, from the sale of products from whales taken under the scientific exemption clause of IWC regulations.

Japan's Whaling for Scientific Purposes

In December 1987, a special meeting of the IWC Scientific Committee convened in Cambridge, England. The purpose of the meeting: to review Japan's new whale research proposal, which included the taking of 300 minke whales in the Antarctic. Catches for scientific purposes are, as mentioned previously, allowed under terms of the 1946 whale convention. However, all whales taken for scientific purposes must be processed as in commercial whaling operations. And it is this requirement that brought forth severe criticism from environmental and animal welfare groups.

After study by the IWC's Scientific Committee, commissioners, and various governments, the United Kingdom put forth a resolution calling for the rejection of Japan's proposal. The resolution was adopted by the IWC. Nevertheless, Japan issued research permits and a fleet, consisting of one factory ship and two whale-catcher boats, sailed for the Antarctic in December 1987. Japan's action brought forth a storm of protests.

Whale conservationists argue that the so-called whale research projects engaged in by Iceland and Japan are thinly disguised efforts at continuing their commercial whaling activities during the moratorium. The Animal Welfare Institute, a Washington, D.C.–based animal protection group, placed a full-page ad in the *New York Times* denouncing Japan's decision to send a fleet to the Antarctic to kill minke whales. The Animal Welfare Institute charged that Japan had sent its whaling fleet to the

Antarctic in defiance of the IWC rejection of the scientific project and the agreement with the United States to end whaling. The ad went on to say that Japan's treachery threatens to destroy more than fifteen years of hard-won whale-conservation measures that have given a short respite to those whales driven to the brink of extinction. The ad also asked: "What will future generations of mankind say of us if we allow a greedy, cynical few to wipe out the species with the most complex brains on our planet?"

Iceland's Research Project

The scientific whaling project put forth by Iceland also came under attack in 1987 and 1988. Environmentalists claimed that whale conservation had been dealt another blow when the United States and Iceland entered into a special agreement regarding Iceland's research project.

After careful review of the Iceland research project, the IWC—at the urging of conservationists—adopted a resolution that called for a halt to the so-called whale research programs. The IWC found that the Icelandic research proposal did not meet the requirements of the IWC research whaling standards. Consequently, the Icelandic government was asked to revoke any and all research permits involving whales.

Under the Pelly Amendment to the Fishermen's Protective Act (1978), the United States may impose embargoes on fish imports from nations that fail to comply with the IWC whale-conservation program. The U.S. commissioner to the IWC was instrumental in the passage of the IWC resolution against research whaling. Such a resolution was necessary if the United States was to impose sanctions against research whaling.

But the special agreement entered into by the United States and Iceland provides that the United States will not impose sanctions for whales killed under the scientific recommendations of the IWC's Scientific Committee.

Whale protectionists speculate that the reason for the leniency shown by the United States on this issue was that Iceland is an important member of NATO. What alarms conservationists is that the bilateral agreement between the United States and Iceland sets a dangerous precedent as far as the conserving of the whales is concerned. Other nations interested in scientific whaling, mainly Japan, Korea, and Norway, are also allies of the U.S. Thus, an important question arises: Will the United States further compromise the whales by entering into future research whaling agreements with these nations?

The United States Reacts
to Japan's Whaling
The United States reacted swiftly to Japan's announcement that it would send a fleet to the Antarctic to kill minke whales. If Japan killed any whales, the United States would consider sanctions under the terms of the Packwood-Magnuson and Pelly amendments, the former entailing a denial of fishing privileges in U.S. waters. Kazuo Shima, councillor to the Japanese Fisheries Agency, blamed the American outcry against Japan's research whaling expedition on racial prejudice. He added that Japan would continue with its research whaling program despite any American threats. "If the United States places sanctions against Japan, we are ready to accept such sanctions."

The Reagan administration supported the IWC moratorium as a matter of policy. However, some environmental groups charged that the State Department often showed too much leniency when it came to enforcing its fishing regulations or in imposing sanctions against violating nations.

Commerce Secretary C. William Verity, Jr., could recommend to the president an embargo on fish imports from Japan. After the secretary initially informed him, the president would then have sixty days in which to inform the Congress if he intended to impose the embargo. If he did not impose an embargo, he would be obliged under the law to explain his decision to Congress.

Trade embargoes are always tricky matters, especially when trade deficits exist between nations. It is difficult to convince industrialists and businesses that whales may be as important as imports and exports. Also, in the case of Japan and its whaling for scientific purposes, an embargo could backfire. The United States sells about three times as much fish to Japan as that country does to the United States. Thus, an embargo on Japanese fish products or other goods could invite retaliation by Japan.

Alan Macnow, a spokesman for the Japanese Institute for Cetacean Research, has pointed out that under terms of the IWC moratorium, an assessment of the world whale population is supposed to be completed by 1990. Japan's 1988 expedition to the Antarctic to hunt minke whales, according to Macnow, was—despite what the United States or other countries might think—designed to contribute to that assessment. Macnow added that "Japan is America's best customer for fish."

Under the terms of the Packwood-Magnuson Amendment, there could be an *automatic* reduction in the amount of fish that Japan could take in U.S. waters. However, this leverage could not be used because Japan had not been given any fishing quotas in American waters in the Pacific in 1988, due to increased American fishing capacity. Therefore, all that the United States was able to do was to warn Japan that by continuing its whaling, it was risking a loss of future fishing rights. Environmentalists and animal welfare organizations called the United States' response a mere slap on the wrist.

More Stringent Penalties Needed?

Environmentalists want the United States to invoke the sanctions of another law, the Pelly Amendment. Under this law, the president could limit or ban the shipment of Japanese fish products to the United States. The Japanese export about $300 million worth of seafood each year.

Campbell Plowden, the whale campaign coordinator for the controversial environmental group, Greenpeace, called the U.S. threat—"if you continue to kill whales, we will not let you fish in our waters"—an "outrageous cop-out." Plowden added that what the president did was "the absolute minimum. It is a clear signal to the Japanese that they can continue their so-called research whaling."

However, the Commerce Department, speaking for the president, said that a total ban on Japanese fishing in American waters was the "best means of encouraging Japan to conform with the International Whaling Commission conservation program." Environmental and animal welfare groups countered with the charge that the United States should have taken a stronger stand and levied stronger penalties because Japan had "double-crossed the United States" when it sent its fleet to the Antarctic to kill minke whales.

The Japanese government, in response to these outcries, has repeated its argument that the whaling expedition to the Antarctic was conducted for scientific purposes. The killing of 300 minke whales, it said, did not violate the IWC moratorium on whaling. Furthermore, argued the Japanese spokesman, the minkes are not an endangered species. Hironao Tanaka, head of the Japanese Fisheries Agency, called the U.S. threat of sanctions "extremely regrettable." He pointed out that scientific whaling was the right of any member nation of the International Whaling Commission.

Japanese officials have long contended that killing nonendangered whales is similar to slaughtering livestock. They also accuse the United States of interfering with Japan's cultural customs and rights. Japanese officials admit that the meat from the minkes killed for scientific purposes would be distributed in Japan. And, they ask,

AN 1853 ENGRAVING SHOWS A WHALING
SCENE OFF THE COAST OF JAPAN.

why not? The Japanese people cannot understand why the killing of a nonendangered species, such as the minke, should cause so much furor and concern. "Americans eat beef," some Japanese say. "Why can't we eat whales?"

Still, the pressure from environmental and animal welfare organizations has increased. The Reagan administration continued to deliberate in 1988 as to what action it should take against Japan. But the antiwhaling groups had no doubts as to the course that should be taken. The president of the World Wildlife Fund, an international conservation organization, issued a statement: "It is outrageous that Japan is now slaughtering hundreds of whales in open defiance of its 1984 agreement with the United States and the International Whaling Commission. It is doubly outrageous that Japan is attempting to justify the action in the name of science."

Dean Wilkenson, wildlife legislative director for Greenpeace, declared that the "message had gone out. Whaling must cease." He added that it "is encouraging that the Commerce Department is following through on the long-standing U.S. policy to end commercial whaling." And Congressman Don Bonker from the state of Washington emphasized that "our government must send a clear and unmistakable message to the government of Japan to stop this slaughter."

SOME IMPORTANT QUESTIONS

The Japanese decision to proceed with their killing of minke whales poses some important questions.

Is it necessary, as the Japanese scientists maintain, to kill minke whales to determine the status of their stocks? Japanese scientists claim that killing minkes is unavoidable, since it is the only certain way to obtain vital data. Observation alone cannot provide the needed data, such as life spans, pregnancy rates, and male-female ratios.

Are the Japanese telling the truth about killing whales solely for scientific purposes? Dean Wilkenson, the Greenpeace spokesman, quickly dismissed the Japanese explanation. "It is clear that Japan never had any intention of honoring its agreements. If killing whales is valuable for scientific learning, the whaling nations missed out on over two million opportunities to learn in the past half-century."

Japanese officials deny engaging in any deception. But they make it very clear that they will resume commercial whaling based on their research findings. As for violating agreements and the IWC moratorium, they claim that they agreed to the ban on whaling only because the United States threatened to reduce allowable fish catches in American waters.

Japanese scientists maintain that the estimate of 250,000 minkes as given by conservation organizations is wrong. They say that scientific evidence supports Japanese estimates of a greater number of these small whales. They repeat that the minkes are not in danger of extinction. Finally, Japanese scientists accuse Americans who have censured them of distorting the issues and of blowing the scientific whaling situation out of proportion. They say the American arguments are invalid because they are based on emotional issues, not on facts.

And that is how matters stand. A big question is this: Will other whaling nations—now observing the moratorium as far as can be verified—decide to follow Japan's action and engage in whaling for "scientific purposes"?

FIVE

BELUGA WHALE
AND DOLPHIN DEATHS

In 1987, more than seventy beluga whales washed up on the shores of the St. Lawrence River and its tributaries. Most of the whales were dead; the rest were dying. Autopsies on the dead whales revealed high levels of chemicals. Among the chemical pollutants found in the whales were DDT; PCBs (polychlorinated biphenyls); a pesticide known as Mirex; various metals, such as mercury and cadmium; and polycyclic aromatic hydrocarbons (similar to chemicals found in cigarettes and known to cause cancer).

The effects of these chemical and metallic pollutants on beluga whales are serious. They have been the cause of various diseases, premature deaths, and—Canadian scientists believe—are responsible for a decline in the birth rate among the belugas, a population now estimated to number fewer than 500 in the St. Lawrence estuary.

Among the diseases found in the beluga whales were bronchial pneumonia, hepatitis, perforated gastric ulcers, pulmonary abcesses, and one case of bladder cancer. The majority of the belugas died from septicemia, or blood poisoning, which resulted from the failure of their immune systems. This failure, it was thought, was brought on by the toxic materials ingested by the whales in the St. Lawrence River and its tributaries. Whales are mammals, and when the chemical pollutants are metabolized, they remain in the cells. The St. Lawrence belugas, according to Dr. Joseph E. Cummins, professor of genetics at the University of Western Ontario, are the "most polluted mammals on earth."

The bottlenose dolphin is commonly seen in coastal waters of the eastern United States. Near the end of 1987, about 470 bottlenose dolphins washed ashore in New Jersey, Delaware, Maryland, Virginia, North Carolina, South Carolina, Georgia, and northern Florida. Their deaths were a mystery. The National Marine Fisheries Service launched an investigation into the cause of the dolphin deaths. Joseph R. Geraci, V.M.D., an expert in marine mammal husbandry and disease, was asked to organize and lead the investigation.

In the early stages of the dolphin die-off, only larger and older dolphins were affected. Later, as the die-off continued, dolphins of all ages and sexes appeared to be affected.

All of the dolphins examined had a variety of internal and external lesions. Some had small blisters and gouges in the skin, which suggested a poxlike viral disease. Other dolphins had large areas of peeling skin, fluid-filled body cavities, and other signs of severe systemic bacterial infections.

Postmortem examinations showed that some dolphins had died a few hours after infection. Others lasted for a longer time, eventually dying from pneumonia, shock, cerebral bleeding, and vascular collapse. Laboratory tests isolated a number of bacteria.

The National Marine Fisheries Service investigating team concluded that bacterial infection was the cause of the dolphin deaths. However, the scientists decided that stress, toxins, and environmental pollutants were also involved.

PLASTIC DEBRIS

All kinds of plastic material enters the sea. Some is tossed overboard from fishing vessels, ocean liners, and other boats. A certain amount reaches the sea by way of runoffs from landfills and sewer systems emptying into the sea. However, the fishing industry has been accused of being the major source of plastic pollution, by way of lost and discarded fishing gear. Some researchers estimate that plastic fishing gear left in the oceans amounts to 100,000 tons each year.

Fishing gear is not the only plastic pollutant charged to the fishing industry. Plastic yokes from beverage six-packs and bags for bait, salt, and ice are found in increasing amounts in coastal regions. Most of these plastic items are traceable to fishing boats or coastal factories.

Such plastic debris has frequently been found in the stomachs of some dolphins. Minke whales have been observed eating plastic heaved into the sea from fishing vessels. Humpback, fin, and right whales have been seen swimming with plastic fishing gear projecting from their mouths. Several pygmy sperm whales and sea turtles died from complications brought on by ingesting plastic material. In some cases, the plastic blocked the animal's intestinal tract. In others, the plastic caused gastric ulceration. Toxic chemicals in the plastic were also a cause of death.

Some fishing companies and ships' captains are

PLASTIC DEBRIS IS
A GLOBAL PROBLEM.

trying to do something about the plastic trash problem. Fisheries representatives have testified before congressional committees and have supported corrective measures. A number of fishing companies are telling their crews to stow plastic and other trash and not heave it overboard. However, plastic debris is a global problem, and a full cleanup needs the cooperation of fishing vessels from all over the world. American fisheries have made a start in the right direction.

OCEANIC POLLUTION A
WORLDWIDE PROBLEM

Marine pollution occurs whenever and wherever human waste materials are dumped into the sea, legally or illegally. Pollution of the sea is not just a recent phenomenon. Since ancient times, the people of nations bordering the sea or its tributaries have cast their sewage and other wastes into the ocean. Flotsam and jetsam—the wreckage of ships and their cargoes found floating in the sea or washed up on shores—were, perhaps, the first visible pollutants. But they posed no serious threat to the ocean environment and its marine life. The sea was able to cope with the flotsam and jetsam for in time, chemical action, scavengers, and the lashing of the winds and currents eventually reduced the trash to relatively small bits of harmless materials.

As civilizations and societies evolved, and large cities appeared along the coasts of the continents, additional and more dangerous kinds of pollutants entered the sea. Cities, farms, and industrial plants dumped their waste products into rivers, bays, estuaries, and coastal waters. Tossing wastes into the sea seemed a natural thing to do, for the sea was a vast region of water, a bottomless waste receptacle with an unlimited ability to absorb and digest all kinds and amounts of waste.

Today, we know that the sea has trouble handling

the vast amounts of wastes dumped into it. True, the sea has an amazing capability to absorb a great deal of waste. However, wastes dumped into the sea must be evenly distributed, not concentrated in certain areas, as recent experience has shown along the New Jersey coast. When nontoxic waste materials are evenly distributed, the ocean's natural forces can break down the pollutants into relatively harmless matter.

Unfortunately for whales and other marine life, heavy concentrations of pollutants occur in many areas throughout the world. Various pollutants are found up to 200 miles (320 km) offshore. These concentrations can be so heavy that the sea's natural forces cannot cope with them. A result is severe damage to marine ecosystems.

OZONE DEPLETION

There is ample evidence to show that certain industrial chemicals—chlorofluorocarbons and halons—are destroying the atmosphere's protective ozone layer. These chemicals are used in the manufacture of refrigerants, foam insulation, and solvents. The destruction of the ozone layer leaves the earth and its life exposed to damage by ultraviolet radiation. And the sea and its life are not exempt.

Dr. Sayed Z. El-Sayed, a professor of oceanography at Texas A&M University, has studied ozone depletion in the Antarctic region. He examined in particular the effects of ultraviolet radiation on marine phytoplankton, microscopic plants that are abundant in the Antarctic Ocean. These tiny marine plants are the food source for krill, the small crustaceans on which the baleen whales feed. El-

THE SEA CANNOT HANDLE THE VAST
AMOUNTS OF WASTE DUMPED INTO IT.

Sayed's experiments showed that increased radiation slowed the process of photosynthesis, the food-making mechanism of the tiny marine plants. When the ultraviolet radiation level was increased by 10 percent, the plants died. The smaller species of phytoplankton, the kind on which krill feed, is especially sensitive to radiation.

A continued increase in ultraviolet radiation—as a result of further destruction of the ozone layer—poses a serious threat to the ocean environment. If anything happens to the krill, the major food supply of the baleen whales and other marine mammals, the sea environment would be mortally wounded. If such a calamity should happen, "we can say good-bye to the whales, to the seals, and to the penguins," according to El-Sayed.

WHALES AND THE OIL INDUSTRY

Most people who watch television or read newspapers are familiar with oil spills in bays and coastal waters. Some oil spills result from malfunctioning offshore oil well operations, damaged tankers, or careless handling by workers. Cargo and passenger ships can discharge waste oil into the sea. Oil also leaks into the sea from refineries and other petroleum-processing sources and through vaporization of petroleum products into the atmosphere. Later, the oil vapor is discharged into the ocean at the air-sea interface—that region where the atmosphere and the sea appear to meet.

In the summer, bowhead whales range in the Beaufort Sea, which stretches from Alaska's North Slope to northwestern Canada, and the frigid waters of the Arctic Ocean. Off the Alaskan north shore lie more oil reserves that are as rich as the supply feeding the Alaskan pipeline to Valdez in the south. Oil companies are drilling in the Beaufort Sea in search of new oil sources. A big question is how these drilling operations will affect the bowhead whales, already an endangered species and an important source of food for Alaskan aborigines.

Will drilling operations interfere with bowhead reproduction? That is a question in search of an answer, particularly in view of the estimated current bowhead population of 7,800 whales.

More research is needed to ascertain the impact of oil-drilling operations on the bowheads and other whales. The behavior of the bowheads in the region of oil-drilling operations is a target of research by the U.S. Minerals Management Service (MMS). MMS scientists believe that increased oil exploration and drilling operations will result in more and heavier ship traffic, thus exposing bowheads and other whales to harassment or injury. MMS officials have not hesitated to stop oil exploration activities when they were dangerous to whales. However, a problem exists as to what constitutes danger or harassment as far as the whales are concerned. Harassment of an endangered species is prohibited under the Endangered Species Act of 1973. Also, scientists fear that an increase in stress and a shortening of the bowhead feeding period due to oil explorations might lead to a reduction in bowhead whale populations.

Although there is some danger of oil being ingested by whales, oil can also pollute plankton. Oil from spills forms a cover, or film, over the surface of the sea. This film blocks sunlight, a necessary ingredient of photosynthesis, or plant-food manufacture. Again, any harm to plankton causes problems for krill, the main food of the baleen whales.

PAPER-PULP POLLUTANTS

Paper-pulp solids and liquids are another source of pollution in the sea. Effluents from paper-manufacturing plants are discharged into rivers, bays, and coastal waters. These substances cause heavy pollution in Puget Sound;

the Atlantic coastal waters off Georgia, South Carolina, and Maine; the Canadian Maritime Provinces; Sweden; and the Soviet Union. This type of oceanic pollution is especially harmful to whales who eat fish, in particular the humpback whale.

Paper-pulp pollutants also have a harmful effect on marine ecosystems. When suspensions of paper-pulp solids are dumped into a bay or estuary, they increase the turbidity of the water, meaning that the water becomes cloudy or opaque, blocking sunlight that is vital to photosynthesis. Thus, in water choked with paper-pulp effluents, a vital process is halted. The result is often lifeless waters.

METALLIC POLLUTANTS

Mercury
We do not often think of metals as pollutants, yet there is strong evidence that certain metals are now posing a threat to the ocean environment and its marine life. One metal now found in bays and estuaries in significant levels is mercury. Toxic levels of mercury have shown up in fish used for human consumption and also eaten by dolphins and humpback and beluga whales.

Lead
Lead is another metal now reaching the sea in increased amounts. The long-range effects of increased levels of lead in the sea—as they relate to whales—are not presently known. Nevertheless, the absence of such data is no excuse for the continued overloading of the sea with this dangerous metal. Its effects on human beings are well-known. We do know that lead is highly toxic to birds.

OFFSHORE OIL RIGS CREATE
HAZARDS FOR SEA LIFE.

Since whales are mammals and equally subject to poisoning, it can be assumed that high levels of lead must be toxic to the whales.

PESTICIDES AND WHALES

Various pesticides are entering the sea. Some of them, particularly DDT, aldrin, dieldrin, and BHC (Benzylhexachloride) are definitely harmful to whales. Aldrin and dieldrin, which accumulate in the fatty tissues of the animal body when taken in through the food chain, are suspected of being cancer-causing agents.

More than 90 percent of these two pesticides is added to soil in cornfields. Soil erosion, caused by wind and water runoff, carries pesticide residues into brooks, creeks, rivers, and eventually into the sea. Even the halting of production of these two pesticides—ordered by the U.S. Environmental Protection Agency more than a decade ago—will not immediately reduce the threat of these pesticides. The sea contains unknown amounts of the two toxic chemicals.

Although the United States has banned the use of these chemicals, Third-World countries are still using them in their agricultural programs. Even though the long-term effects of these pesticides are not fully known, we do know that they pose a threat to human and marine life. A variety of pesticides are found in fish and shellfish, and it is reasonable to assume that they can be found in some whales. These chemicals cause cancer, mutations, and deformities.

Another toxic chemical that has gained notoriety is known as PCB (Polychlorinated biphenyl). It is estimated that 25 percent of the world production of PCB eventually leaks into the environment. Of this 25 percent, 20 percent enters the atmosphere and is ultimately transported to the sea by global winds. The remaining 5 percent goes into rivers and works its way into the waters of the continental shelves, which contain the world's richest fishing grounds. These regions of abundant fish are also the feeding grounds of some whales, notably the humpback whale and the bottlenose dolphin.

BACTERIA AND VIRUSES IN THE SEA

The beleaguered sea environment must also contend with bacteria and viruses flushed into the sea by way of raw sewage and other solid wastes. Bacteria and viruses capable of causing human and animal diseases have been isolated in bays and coastal waters. A case in point is the death of the beluga whales in the St. Lawrence River.

RADIOACTIVE WASTES

Another growing source of danger for whales is radioactive wastes. Nuclear testing, mainly by the United States and the Soviet Union, is the primary source of artificial radionuclides found in the sea. The present concentration of artificially produced radionuclides, according to the Food and Agriculture Organization of the United Nations, is 109 curies. (The curie is used to measure the level of radioactivity.)

Scientists have found that most of the radioactive pollutants remain on the surface of the sea. They are restricted to the Northern Hemisphere, since most of the nuclear testing is done in that portion of the world. Some whales undoubtedly pass through these radioactive areas on their migrations.

PROTECTION OF THE MARINE ENVIRONMENT

Ocean dumping in the United States is regulated under the authority of the Marine Protection, Research, and

Sanctuaries Act of 1972. This law bans the dumping of high-level radioactive wastes, chemicals, pesticides, and biological warfare agents in the sea. Other wastes, including sewage (but not dredged materials), may be dumped into the sea at designated sites by permit only. Permits are issued subject to certain regulations established by the U.S. Environmental Protection Agency. Research and the establishment of marine sanctuaries (sea areas where no dumping is allowed) are the province of the National Oceanic and Atmospheric Administration.

Since the Marine Protection Act became law, ocean dumping has increased. Critics charge that some of the permits issued are not in the best interests of the marine environment. Critics also charge that enforcement of the law is often weak and sometimes nonexistent. This claim was validated in 1988 when vacationers along New Jersey's coast found their vacations ruined because beaches were closed as a result of contamination by sewage sludge and medical wastes from hospitals. New Jersey's coastal contamination brought forth demands for stricter enforcement of ocean-dumping regulations. Despite state and federal efforts to put an end to ocean dumping, environmentalists say the end to ocean dumping is not in sight.

The U.S. Congress has enacted other laws for regulating the dumping of wastes and pollutants into the sea. The Outer Continental Shelf Act provides for the prompt removal of oil spills along the continental shelf on the eastern coast. The Deep Water Ports Act prohibits seagoing vessels from discharging oil into the ocean. The Intervention on the High Seas Act deals with materials

ROTTING FISH IN RIVERS AND SEAS
ARE EVIDENCE OF THE GROWING
PROBLEM OF POLLUTION.

discharged into the sea by ships that have been damaged, or from released cargoes. These laws provide potential protection for the ocean. But they are poorly supervised and weakly enforced.

The U.S. Coast Guard, as the marine police authorized to deal with illegal dumping, has not done a good job of enforcing the laws, according to environmentalists. Coast Guard officials respond to the criticism by saying they do not have enough boats or personnel for the task. Illicit ocean dumpers—who want to avoid paying landfill fees—use sophisticated equipment to monitor the whereabouts of Coast Guard ships. The vastness of the ocean environment to be covered by the Coast Guard makes the task difficult, sometimes impossible.

Ecologists are greatly concerned about the continued pollution of the ocean environment. Scarcely an Atlantic coast city or town is safe from contamination of its fish and shellfish. Contaminated fish are consumed by humpback, fin, and right whales, by harbor porpoises, and by the Atlantic whitesided and bottlenose dolphins that travel up and down the Atlantic coastal waters.

Pacific coastal waters are also polluted; contaminated waters stretch from Puget Sound (a heavily polluted waterway) south to Baja California. The gray whales follow the Pacific coastline on their migrations. From June to October, the gray whales congregate in the Chukchi Sea between Alaska and the Soviet Union. On their southern migration, they travel through the Bering Strait, then follow the Alaskan coastline south to the Canadian coast, and from there down past Seattle, through heavily polluted waters until they reach the lagoons and coastal waters of Baja California.

It is estimated that 75 percent of the nation's population lives on or close to the seacoasts. Since coastal population growth will undoubtedly continue, and whales and other marine life will continue to have to swim through polluted coastal waters on their annual migrations, ocean pollution is unquestionably a major problem for the future. Although pollution has not yet claimed the number of whale deaths that commercial whaling has in the past, it is a definite threat to whale stocks, especially those struggling to recover from their losses.

SIX

Most people have seen dolphins and porpoises, either on television, in the sea off coastlines, or in seaquariums. These agile and graceful whales have fascinated scientists and others for quite some time. A large store of knowledge about the biology and behavior of dolphins and porpoises has been gained by many studying the animals in seaquariums such as Marineland of the Pacific Research Laboratory, the New York Aquarium, and the National Marine Laboratory at Kaneohe Bay in Hawaii. One important finding of all this research is that these little whales are highly intelligent and friendly mammals.

It is their intelligence, friendliness, and seeming kinship with humans that make the often-wanton death of porpoises and dolphins so hard for many people to take. Thousands of dolphins and porpoises die each year, either as a result of being trapped in American tuna nets or in the gill nets of Japanese fishermen. The U.S. Marine Mammal Commission refers to these deaths as the "incidental take of marine mammals in the course of commercial fishing operations." Environmentalists and animal protection groups call the deaths unnecessary slaughters. In 1987, the tuna industry was responsible for the deaths of more than 14,000 porpoises.

More than a hundred tuna boats sail from southern California ports. These boats head for the waters of the eastern tropical Pacific, with their great schools of yellowfin tuna. Tuna fishing is a very competitive business. There is competition between nations, companies, and even individual boats. Using modern, sophisticated equipment, tuna boat captains make every effort to locate schools of tuna, as well as the eastern spinner and spotted porpoises, two species that feed on the yellowfin tuna. When the tuna are located, the boats zero in on them and cast out their huge purse seine nets:

Imagine that you are aboard a tuna boat. A lookout is perched high on a mast. He shades his eyes and peers out over the sea swells, searching for signs of the profitable tuna. Suddenly, he leans forward in stiff attention. Dead ahead is the sign he was looking for: porpoises leaping in and out of the water.

"Tuna ahead!" sings out the lookout.

The tuna boat captain calls for more speed, and the boat plows through the choppy sea, bearing down on the porpoises and tuna below them.

As the boat nears the porpoises, you stare down into water and notice a dark mass just below the surface and the gamboling porpoises. The mass you see is a tightly packed school of yellowfin tuna.

A net skiff is now launched. It speeds in a wide circle around the porpoises and tuna, towing a half-mile long purse seine net. The motorboat completes its mission, and both tuna and porpoises are encircled by the huge net. You watch as the net is drawn tighter around the tuna and porpoises.

Many of the trapped porpoises panic. They dash into the sides of the net in a frantic effort to escape. Some of them are caught under the mass of tuna, like fallen people in a stampeding mob. If they become entangled in the net, they are unable to surface in order to breathe and may suffocate. Distress whistles fill the air.

The trapped porpoises struggle frantically to reach the surface of the sea. A fisherman throws some fire-crackers into the water to frighten the porpoises, hoping they will move to the back of the net. But this does not happen, and the porpoises churn the water in the net into white foam. Their haunting cries rise up from the mass of tuna. As the net is lifted up from the sea, you see porpoises snared in the netting. Some are twisting and struggling, others hang still like dead soldiers on barbed wire. Later, the fishermen separate the porpoises from the tuna, tossing the dead, stunned, or dying whales back into the sea.

A scene similar to the foregoing was reported by a marine biologist affiliated with the Earth Island Institute, a leading advocate for saving dolphins and porpoises based in San Francisco. The biologist signed on as a crewmember on a Latin American tuna boat. This undercover biologist witnessed the killing of porpoises much in the manner previously described.

THE TUNA-PORPOISE ISSUE

In 1986, the U.S. tuna fleet alone killed 20,500 porpoises. Since this number was so high, it was prohibited from fishing for tuna by setting nets on porpoises. However,

A NEWBORN DOLPHIN AND
ITS MOTHER DELIGHT
VISITORS AT A SEAQUARIUM.

SPOTTED DOLPHINS ENCOUNTER MANY HAZARDS—
INCLUDING GETTING TRAPPED IN TUNA-FISHING NETS.

the porpoise kill in 1987 was lower than in 1986, and the prohibition was lifted.

Tuna found with porpoises tend to be larger than those not followed by the small whales. Fishermen know this, and that is why they cast their purse seine nets where the porpoises are. Large tuna bring a better price than do the smaller fish. Consequently, the porpoises associated with the larger tuna have the misfortune of "getting in the way" of the fishermen after the big tunas.

The tuna industry has complained that the methods used to estimate the number of porpoises killed are flawed and that the true kill of porpoises has been overestimated. In response to this complaint, the National Marine Fisheries Service initiated a study of the issue. The service decided to provide 100-percent observer coverage of tuna operations in 1987 and 50-percent coverage in 1988. It also considered passing some regulations regarding the performance of individual tuna-fishing vessels and captains in the tuna industry.

The American Tunaboat Association strongly objected to these proposed regulations, especially those dealing with the performance of tuna boat captains. A spokesman for the association stated that there was no need for the National Marine Fisheries Service to regulate "skipper performance," since there was a regulatory body already in existence for such a purpose: the Expert Skippers Panel. Any tuna boat captain performing poorly or one who had too large a porpoise kill could be brought before the panel, which would review the circumstances surrounding a situation where an overkill of porpoises occurred. This panel would also consider other relevant factors, such as the captain's experience.

FOREIGN TUNA FLEETS

U.S. tuna fishermen have complained that any reduction by them in porpoise deaths is offset by the high kill rates of foreign tuna fleets. If more progress is to be made in reducing the porpoise kills, foreign tuna fleets will have to comply with regulations and restraints similar to those observed by the U.S. fleet.

Congress enacted an amendment to the Marine Mammal Protection Act, which requires that any nation exporting tuna to the United States must provide documentary evidence that it has a program aimed at reducing the incidental take of porpoises during tuna operations. Furthermore, such a program must be comparable to that of the United States. Also, the average rate of incidental kills must be comparable to that of the U.S. tuna fleet. Failure to meet these requirements may result in a ban on the import of tuna and tuna products from the offending nation.

The U.S. stand on incidental killing of porpoises by foreign tuna fleets has caused some confusion. For one thing, there is the question of what a comparable kill is. Clarification is also needed for the porpoise protection programs of foreign nations. Must they be the same as that of the United States or just equivalent? These and other measures regulating the killing of porpoises by foreign tuna fleets remain unresolved. Environmentalists complain that the discrepancy between the kills made by the U.S. tuna fleet and those of foreign nations is still too high.

DALL'S PORPOISES AND JAPANESE FISHERMEN

Among the marine mammals taken in Japanese high seas salmon driftnets are Dall's porpoises. These small whales are trapped in the nets in what is known as the U.S. Exclusive Economic Zone (EEZ) in the North Pacific Ocean. Prior to 1987, Japanese salmon fishermen were allowed to take a total of 5,500 Dall's porpoises each year within the EEZ. A new permit would have allowed Jap-

BEFORE 1987, DEAD PORPOISES LINED UP
ON JAPANESE DOCKS WERE A FREQUENT SIGHT.

anese fishermen a total take of 6,039 porpoises until 1990. However, litigation over the decision to issue the permit effectively voided the permit and prevented this fishing in 1988.

The estimated annual taking of porpoises and dolphins in fishing nets exceeds 100,000 each year, which includes American and foreign tuna operations. The killing of the small whales—incidental or not—is the largest slaughter of marine mammals in the world. Critics of the killings maintain that existing laws are not being enforced. They charge that some tuna fishermen actually net the porpoises on purpose as they sweep their tuna nets through the seas. Tuna fishermen deny this charge and say they cannot help it if the porpoises get caught in their nets. People want tuna, and the only practical way of catching the fish is by use of the large purse seine nets.

The Earth Island Institute brought suit against the U.S. government in 1986. It sought more rigid enforcement of existing laws, greater protection of the dolphins and porpoises, and the banning of all tuna from boats guilty of killing the small whales.

The institute also called for a boycott of all canned tuna. Although most porpoises die in the netting of the yellowfin tuna, the institute recommended that all kinds of tuna be banned. By such an action, according to the institute, the big tuna canners, such as Star-Kist, Carnation, Chicken of the Sea, and Bumble Bee, will get the message. Many ecologists and conservationists say that appeals to morality or animal protection do not work with the big industries. The only way to get results is by hitting the fishing companies and canners in their pocketbooks.

Ordinarily, the right to conduct a business as one sees fit—providing no laws are violated—is a traditional American right. But, according to environmentalists, the tuna industry has been killing whales, a natural resource that belongs to all the world. Although the tuna fishermen have the right to take tuna, they do not have the right to kill thousands of dolphins and porpoises, incidentally or otherwise. Since tuna fishermen do kill the small whales, environmentalists and animal protection groups believe the tuna industry should be held accountable. It should not be permitted to flout laws or block porpoise- and dolphin-protection programs.

Conservationists admit that the U.S. tuna industry has reduced its killing of dolphins and porpoises. But they charge that little is being done in the case of foreign tuna fleets. No embargoes or sanctions have been placed on the importation of fish and fish products from nations that fail to meet American marine conservation standards. The nations operating tuna boats in the eastern tropical Pacific Ocean are Panama, Costa Rica, Ecuador, Mexico, and Spain.

Senator John Kerry, Democrat of Massachusetts, stated in 1988 that "foreign tuna fleets in the eastern tropical Pacific are killing over 100,000 porpoises a year, and our government agencies have done little to implement the changes designed to address the problem." Kerry was referring to the amendment to the Marine Mammal Protection Act that permits the United States to ban the importation of fish and fish products from any nation failing to reduce the incidental killing of porpoises. Kerry added that the U.S. Commerce and State departments have shown nothing but "malaise," or a feeling of discomfort, about the killing of the porpoises.

Spokespeople for the National Marine Fisheries Service say that it is not easy to solve the problem. It is very difficult to draw up rules and regulations for a problem that is so complex and involves a number of foreign nations. Threatening these nations with embargoes or boycotts would be futile, according to the Fisheries Service. Threatened nations would simply take their tuna catches somewhere else, such as Asia or Europe. Consequently, the American fish markets would suffer, for the American people consume a lot of tuna.

LARGE WHALES
AND FISHING NETS

Dolphins and porpoises are not the only whales being trapped in fishing nets. Humpback whales and an occasional finback, minke, or right whale become entangled in fishing nets off the coast of Newfoundland. Humpbacks swim and feed in coastal waters, and some of them get snarled in the large fishing nets spread in the sea by the more than 25,000 Newfoundland fishermen.

No two whales are trapped in the same way, according to Professor Jon Lien, an animal behaviorist at Memorial University in Newfoundland. Some whales are what Lien calls "bridled"; that is, parts of fishing nets are caught in their mouths, restricting the whale's ability to open and close its cavernous mouth. Sometimes a whale's fin is hooked in a net; other times a net gets wrapped around a tail or flukes. And in still other cases, whales are trapped by nets tangled on heads, fins, and flukes.

Labrador fishermen are not whale lovers. They regard the whales that swim into their nets as pests and vandals. A severely damaged net can spell disaster for a Labrador fisherman, whose average earnings are less than $7,000 a year. The Newfoundland fishing season is short—no more than three months. A damaged net can put a fisherman out of business for a season. Newfoundland fishermen have lost as much as a total of $3 million a year in damaged nets and income.

Professor Lien advises fishermen on how to untangle a whale from a net. He also helps fishermen do the job. Before the professor became involved in freeing whales from nets, fishermen simply waited for a whale to work itself free or die. This procedure took some time. Also, dead whales sink to the bottom of the sea, taking nets with them. It may be a week or more before their bodies surface again.

Most trapped whales can be freed without too much trouble, depending on the degree of entanglement. Professor Lien uses specially designed knives and grapples to do the job. Most whales caught in nets are eager to have the netting and ropes removed from their mouths and bodies. "Whales are great big sissies," says Lien. "They really want the nets out of their mouths."

What draws the humpback whales to the fishing areas are the schools of capelin, the small smeltlike fish that are used as bait to catch cod. But the bait attracts both cod and whales. A result is a clash between whales and fishermen. This problem has increased over the past five years. One of the reasons for an increase in net entanglements is that there are more nets in the waters off Newfoundland than before. The more nets, the more collisions by whales. It is a vicious cycle, and fishermen are not happy with the situation.

There are some other reasons for the increase in net entanglements. Professor Lien and other marine experts believe that a shortage of capelin far out in the sea brings the humpbacks, fins, and minkes closer into shore, where the fishing nets are spread. Another reason is that there is an increase in the populations of these three whale stocks. It is believed that the growth of these whale stocks has resulted from the discontinuation of whaling by the United States in 1971 and Canada in 1972.

Some fishing interests and fishermen have called for a limited hunting season on the whales visiting the Newfoundland waters. If the number of whales coming into the fishing regions can be reduced, so can the entanglements in nets and the resultant loss of fishing gear and income. But the International Whaling Commission moratorium on commercial whaling is still in effect and cannot be changed to accommodate the Newfoundland fishing industry. In addition, the humpback and fin whales remain endangered species, despite any slight increase in their stocks.

Fishermen continue to complain about their whale problem. Some think that shooting trapped whales would ease their workload. But shooting a whale rarely kills the animal, though it does cause injury and pain to the whale. Injured whales can swim amok, doing great damage to fishing gear and posing a threat to small boats and human beings. In one case of whale shooting off the Newfoundland coast, a whale went berserk. The frenzied animal swam along the shore, running into many nets and dragging them along in its mad flight.

Several suggestions for reducing whale and fishing net collisions have been put forward. One is the use of sonar devices that could be attached to the fishing nets. It is believed that the sounds given off by the device would warn a whale away from a net. At the same time, the sounds would not scare off the cod.

Some Canadian fishermen have asked the Canadian government to compensate them for their losses. The Canadian government did set up a program for fishing-gear replacement. Special depots were established at which a fisherman can buy a whole cod net or parts to replace those damaged by whales. Thus, using these depots, fishermen can get right back into business instead of waiting for repairs to a damaged net.

It has also been suggested that a change in the location of cod nets could help avoid collisions by whales. Some cod locations seem to attract more whales than others. The idea, according to some authorities, is to put the cod nets where the fishing is good but the whale activity low.

Some authorities recommend fishing with trawl lines. Fishing trawls have many short lines attached to a long line at regular intervals. Each short line has a hook usually baited with squid. Trawls are set on the bottom of the sea by means of a small anchor at each end of the long line. The underwater trawl lines are marked by buoys. Later, they are hauled up to a boat for the removal of the fish. Each line is 50 fathoms, or 300 feet, long and there may be as many as thirty lines set altogether. Whales rarely get caught in trawl lines.

Finally, in some of the Newfoundland coastal waters, humpback and fin whales are plentiful for only a short time. They are most numerous at the peak of the capelin season. Therefore, it might be advantageous to encourage fishermen to go elsewhere during the period the whales and capelin are together. Whether the fishermen will agree to this kind of arrangement remains to be seen. Since the clash between Newfoundland fishermen and whales promises to become more intense—as whale stocks increase—all possible suggestions for easing the situation should be examined and tested.

SEVEN

Today, "Save the Whales" is a slogan in a number of countries. The United States has been the leader in the crusade to save the whales. Scientists, government officials, various federal and state agencies, many environmental and animal protection groups, and ordinary people have all become involved in the plight of the whales.

The moratorium on commercial whaling, imposed by the International Whaling Commission, is being observed by most nations. The halt in commercial whaling is aimed at giving endangered whale species a chance to replenish their depleted stocks. But is this possible for all the endangered species? Only time will tell.

During the whaling year of 1930–31, whalers from various nations killed close to 30,000 blue whales, the largest of the baleen group. Today, the blue whale population is estimated at 12,000. This number may be too small for complete recovery.

A major problem with the blue whales, according to marine biologists, is that their few numbers make it difficult for males and females to find one another to mate and reproduce in the vast stretches of the world's oceans. The blue whales have been protected since 1965, yet there is little evidence of any increase in numbers.

Conservationists and environmental agencies continue to call for more stringent protective measures for the whales and more efficient management programs. Newspapers and magazines carry pleas and demands to save the whales. Advertisements aimed at making concerned readers aware of what they can do to help the whales—from writing to government officials to boycotting products from nations engaged in whale killing— often occupy full pages in major newspapers. Television also promotes the protection of whales by running documentaries, educational films, and news items about whales.

Why all the fuss about whales? Are they so vital to human existence? Why are more and more people becoming concerned with these giant seagoing mammals?

People have various reasons for what they think or do. In the case of the whales, most people believe that these great sea beasts are an integral part of our natural heritage—a main strand in the web of life—and as such should be preserved, protected, and managed wisely.

NATIONAL MARINE
FISHERIES SERVICE

The Marine Mammal Protection Act of 1972 delegates authority and responsibility for most species of oceanic mammals (whales and seals) to the National Marine Fisheries Service (NMFS). The NMFS, therefore, is the government agency responsible for the conservation and protection of all whales in U.S. waters.

Under the provisions of the Marine Mammal Protection Act, whales and dolphins may be taken for scientific research, public display in seaquariums or marine laboratories, and incidentally in commercial fishery activities. Also, native North Americans—Eskimos and Aleuts— may take limited numbers of whales for subsistence and production of handicrafts in keeping with their customs and traditions.

The NMFS can grant or deny permits to take whales and dolphins. The agency also carries out research and management programs. It enforces the Marine Mammal Protection Act and cooperates with other nations in whale conservation and management programs. The NMFS also cooperates with private environmental and animal protection groups, such as Greenpeace, the Sierra Club, the National Wildlife Federation, and the World Wildlife Fund.

One of the controversial whale management programs of the NMFS concerns the taking of porpoises in tuna fishing operations. (The NMFS uses the term *porpoise* to include both dolphins and porpoises and to avoid confusing the dolphin whale with the dolphin fish.) The NMFS allows a total take of 20,500 porpoises by American tuna fishermen in a season. This incidental dolphin take is subject to specific rules, regulations, guidelines, and monitoring by agency observers.

Regardless of the rules and regulations, environmentalists say that the allowable take of 20,500 porpoises is too much. This number is subject to review, and it may be that pressure from environmentalists will result in a reduction of the quota in future years. At this time, there is no way to prevent some porpoises from being trapped in tuna nets.

Conflicts and hostilities between certain fisheries and environmental organizations sometimes reach high emotional levels. One such organization—Greenpeace USA— has organized protests and taken drastic action against the killing of whales.

GREENPEACE
AND THE WHALES

Greenpeace was founded in 1970. This organization is composed of conservationists who believe in direct action, rather than in passive or verbal protests.

Greenpeace achieved world notice when, in 1986, some of its activist members placed their boat between whales and a Norwegian chaser boat in what Greenpeace called the Moby Dick campaign to halt commercial whaling. Greenpeace activists actually lassoed the harpoon of a Norwegian boat.

Through its efforts, Greenpeace has brought the plight of the whales to the attention of the world. In its campaign to save the whales, Greenpeace activists and boats have confronted whalers from Japan, the Soviet Union, Iceland, Norway, Peru, and Spain. Films showing Greenpeace activists placing themselves between explosive harpoons and whales have dramatically directed public attention to the issue of whaling.

Greenpeace has also sent teams to investigate and document pirate whaling. Pirate whaling is the killing of whales by nations or companies without regard for International Whaling Commission or national regulations. These whale pirates ignore quotas and regulations against the taking of protected species. Greenpeace teams have exposed pirate whaling by Peru, Taiwan, Japan, and the Philippines. Their efforts along these lines have led to the termination of some of these illegal whaling operations.

Greenpeace has also been active within the International Whaling Commission and has brought whale issues before the U.S. Congress. The organization has campaigned to convince government officials of the need to protect the whales. Greenpeace opposes the IWC rule that allows whaling for scientific purposes. Greenpeace members flood the officials of whaling nations with letters and postcards demanding a cessation of their whaling

GREENPEACE HAS BROUGHT THE PLIGHT OF THE
WHALE TO THE ATTENTION OF THE WORLD.

activities. Greenpeace has taken the United States to court for its failure to impose sanctions on Japan when that nation violated the moratorium on whaling. All of Greenpeace's actions have been aimed at ending the commercial slaughter of whales and "preserving these wonderful animals for future generations, and protecting the delicate balance of marine ecosystems."

INTERNATIONAL WHALING COMMISSION

After its establishment in 1946, the International Whaling Commission functioned more or less as a cartel geared to stabilize whale-oil prices. There was no attempt to conserve whale stocks. In fact, during the first ten years of the IWC's existence, whaling quotas were set so high that nations rushed to sea to compete for the whales. This period was known as the Whaling Olympics. It peaked in the 1961–62 season when more than 76,000 whales were killed. Despite clear evidence that certain species, especially the blue whale, were severely depleted, the IWC failed to take any corrective action.

Pressure on the IWC
When the United States ceased whaling in 1971 and Canada in 1972—and when public awareness of the plight of the whales heightened—the IWC was forced to consider protecting endangered species. When non-whaling nations joined the IWC—as was their right—the whaling nations no longer had a majority in the commission. And in 1982, the IWC passed by a vote of 25–7 the moratorium on commercial whaling to begin in the 1986 season.

IWC Current Programs
Some IWC-member nations have implemented major research programs that include the sampling of whales

caught under special permits that the IWC allows them to issue. The commission has sponsored a second International Decade of Cetacean Research that will concentrate on sighting surveys of Antarctic minke whales. The IWC Scientific Committee is also engaged in an in-depth study of the status of whale stocks as they pertain to management objectives.

Flaws in the IWC Structure

There are several flaws, or loopholes, in the IWC structure, which were built in when the commission was established.

One is that any nation can exempt itself from a decision or ruling by the IWC simply by filing an objection within ninety days. The Soviet Union and Norway have taken advantage of this ruling and continue to exercise their objection to the 1982 moratorium on commercial whaling.

Another weakness of the IWC is the provision that allows any nation to issue permits to kill whales for scientific purposes. Such permits are not subject to the quotas established by the commission. The only requirement is that the nation notify the IWC of and submit for review any permits that have been issued.

Finally, the IWC lacks the power to enforce its rules and regulations. The commission, like the United Nations, is impotent when it comes to a nation that defies its rules or mandates. The IWC cannot impose sanctions or seize ships of those nations that ignore or violate its guidelines and regulations.

U.S. Programs

Since the U.S. fishing industry no longer hunts whales, research efforts are concentrated on the dolphin and porpoise problem. One such research program involves a study of the trends in the abundance of porpoise stocks that are killed in tuna-fishing operations. For example, an important question is whether the stocks are high or low. The research is being conducted by the NMFS Southwest Fisheries Center. After this research is completed, the status of porpoise stocks will be reevaluated.

NMFS scientists are also gathering data on the physical and biological environment in which the porpoises live. Such data center on the surface temperature of the sea, salinity, and fluorescence. Water samples to test for nutrient and chlorophyll values are being collected. These data will be used to figure out the distribution of porpoises in the eastern tropical Pacific. It is expected that the data will also help marine biologists to predict how large-scale environmental factors—such as temporary ocean warming, called El Nino—affect the encounters between porpoises and tuna boats.

Another project includes a study of the life histories of porpoises collected by observers on tuna boats. Such studies involve an analysis of specific changes in the porpoise growth rate, age of sexual maturity, pregnancy rate, and the sex ratio of porpoises killed in fishing operations. Scientists have found that changes in the sex ratio of spotted dolphins correlate with changes in fishing operations. All of these research projects will prove invaluable in analyzing the effect of tuna operations on different species of dolphins and porpoises.

Another project aimed at studying the decimation of dolphins along the East Coast was started in 1988. The Office of Naval Research and the National Marine Fisheries Service have each contributed $50,000 to the project. A task force headed by Dr. Joseph R. Geraci, professor of veterinary medicine at the University of Guelph near Toronto, will examine the deaths of dolphins cast up on the eastern shores. More than 800 dolphins have been washed ashore on the southern New Jersey beaches. The cause of the deaths is unknown, although scientists believe the dolphin immune system is involved.

Stranded Whale
Rescue Programs

The National Marine Fisheries Service, in cooperation with private environmental organizations and individuals, operates a marine mammal stranding network. Whale strandings are recorded with a regional coordinator. Stranded whales are removed from beaches as quickly as possible, since they must get back into their watery environment to live. The program has achieved considerable success in saving the lives of whales. One such rescue operation involved a humpback whale named Humphrey that wandered into the San Francisco–Sacramento River delta. Humphrey was finally led out to sea twenty-four days later by the combined efforts of various public agencies, volunteer groups, and concerned individuals. Almost a year later, Humphrey was sighted in the gulf of the Farallon Islands off the coast of California. Many humpback whales have been studied for unique markings and later recognized. The stranded whale program is an important conservation measure.

In the early summer of 1988, a humpback whale entered the Hudson River. The whale—named Henry after Henry Hudson, explorer of the Hudson River—forced two ferry boats off course. Some people in a pleasure boat pursued the whale, thus complicating a hazardous situation. Henry was eventually turned around by the U.S. Coast Guard and urged back to sea. The whale was believed to be an immature humpback. Young whales are very curious and will swim close to shore, even entering harbors. Fortunately, this whale was returned to the sea without injury, although there was speculation that the whale may have been sick from feeding in the polluted Hudson River.

Three young California gray whales found themselves trapped in deep ice in the Beaufort Sea off Point Barrow, Alaska, in the fall of 1988. The desperate plight of the three whales—bloodied and exhausted from their

SKINDIVERS ATTEMPT TO RESCUE A HUMPBACK WHALE
STRANDED ON A ROCKY BEACH IN CALIFORNIA.

struggles to obtain air—drew international attention and cooperation.

Putu, Siku, and Kanik, as the Eskimo whalers called the three stranded whales, became the focus of an unusual and costly rescue effort that brought together some unlikely allies. The Alaskan National Guard, an oil-industry service company, environmentalists, workers from an oil company, a marine biologist from the U.S. Fisheries Service, and the crews of two Soviet icebreaker ships were involved in the rescue of the icebound whales.

Eskimo whalers used chain saws to cut out blocks of ice to widen the air holes occupied by the whales. A barge was sent from Prudhoe Bay, 200 miles (320 km) east of Point Barrow, to splinter ice from the open sea to the pool containing the trapped gray whales. But the barge failed to break the ice.

Some whaling captains thought it best to shoot the trapped whales and put them out of their misery. The meat and blubber could be given to the Eskimos. However, this solution was quickly rejected, for the three whales had now become important to people all over the world when their struggle to stay alive was shown on countless television sets.

For more than a week, the fate of the whales was in doubt. It was obvious that they were tiring from their constant bobbing to the surface for gulps of air. And when one of the whales disappeared and was presumed dead, the big question was whether an open sea lane could be chopped or cut to the Beaufort Sea in time to save the remaining two whales.

The rescue operation was now proving to be extremely costly, as high as $1 million. Was it worth this to try to save the two trapped whales? Ron Morris, the biologist who served as coordinator for the rescue, had some doubts. At one point in the rescue operations, he stated that if polar bears tried to get at the whales, he would not interfere but would let nature take its course.

BIOLOGISTS, ENVIRONMENTALISTS, AND VOLUNTEERS
STRUGGLED TO RESCUE GRAY WHALES TRAPPED IN
THE ICE-CLOGGED BEAUFORT SEA.

The arrival of two Soviet icebreakers eventually settled the matter. The ships plowed a channel through the thick ice from the Beaufort Sea to the pools that had trapped the whales for almost two weeks. There were sighs of relief all over the world when the two surviving whales pushed through chunks of ice in the new channel on their way to the open sea. Everyone wished the whales good luck on their long journey south to Baja California and the wintering lagoons of the gray whales.

Alaskan Natives and Bowhead Whales

Bowhead whales are an endangered species. However, Alaskan natives are permitted to hunt them for subsistence purposes—that is, for food and for handicraft items for sale. Catch limits of the bowheads are set by the International Whaling Commission. Both the U.S. Endangered Species Act and the Marine Mammal Protection Act allow natives to take endangered species, subject to certain regulations and catch limits.

The National Marine Fisheries Service has the primary responsibility for managing the bowhead whales in the U.S. EEZ. Some other agencies are also involved. They include the state of Alaska, the Alaska Eskimo Whaling Commission, the North Slope Borough, and the Minerals Management Service.

Whale Conservation Organizations

The whales now have many friends and protectors. Thousands of people belong to environmental and animal protection organizations that campaign for the protection and wise management of the world's whales. These organizations range from the activist type, such as Greenpeace, and fund-raising groups, such as the Fund for Animals, to whale-education groups, such as the Center for Environmental Education.

Whale Research and Conservation • This organization, located in Alameda, California, promotes whale research and conservation. The agency also sponsors educational projects, supervises whale-watching activities, and sends a representative to International Whaling Commission meetings.

The Whale Center • The Whale Center, located in San Francisco, sponsors whale-conservation projects. Some of the organization's goals are to establish whale sanctuaries, protect whale habitats, promote whale research, and conduct whale-watching expeditions off the California coast. The organization has done some original surveys of gray whales in the waters of Baja California.

U.S. Marine Mammal Commission • This Washington, D.C.–based agency was established by Congress to oversee the protection and conservation of all marine mammals. The commission conducts research on marine mammals and makes recommendations on federal programs that affect marine mammals.

National Oceanic and Atmospheric Administration

This federal agency is the parent agency of the NMFS, which administers the program for the management, protection, and conservation of endangered marine species. It also controls the use of whales and other marine mammals for public display. The agency issues permits for the capture of marine mammals, including endangered species intended for scientific research.

Other Conservation Groups

Other, but no less important, groups involved in whale conservation include the Sierra Club, the Audubon Society, the National Wildlife Federation, and the Whale Protection Fund.

MARINE SANCTUARIES

The United States controls 2.2 million square miles (5.7 million sq km) of ocean environment. Included in this vast oceanic region are widely diversified marine ecosystems. These range from the unique coral reefs of the Florida Keys and the Grand Banks of the Atlantic Ocean to the Beaufort Sea off the northeastern coast of Alaska. To many marine biologists and conservationists, it seemed this great ocean territory needed to be protected from damage by human activities. Consequently, in 1972, the U.S. Congress passed the Marine Protection, Research, and Sanctuaries Act, which authorized the establishment of the National Marine Sanctuary Program.

The fundamental purpose of the program is to conserve and protect the major marine areas through proper management, research, and education. An individual marine sanctuary does not concentrate on one order, family, or species of marine mammal. The focus is on preserving and managing all marine resources within a sanctuary.

Environmentalists hailed the establishment of the National Marine Sanctuary Program as a long-overdue conservation measure. However, the program's promise and potential as a marine mammal protection effort has not lived up to some expectations. What should have been a workable wildlife management measure floundered and became bogged down in a maze of controversy and political maneuvers. A lack of coordination among various state and federal marine and coastal management programs compounded the problems of the Marine Sanctuary Program.

Two marine sanctuary sites involving whales were designated under the provisions of the program. One is

SCIENTISTS WATCH AS PILOT WHALES BEACHED ON CAPE COD ARE PREPARED FOR A RETURN TO THE SEA.

the Gulf of the Farallones, originally named the Point Reyes/Farallon Islands National Marine Sanctuary. This marine sanctuary encompasses 948 square miles (2,465 sq km) and is located northwest of San Francisco. Humpback whales—and sometimes a blue whale—may be seen in this oceanic sanctuary.

The waters surrounding the Hawaiian Islands were also designated as a marine sanctuary. The endangered humpback whales breed and calve in this island region. However, after detailed studies and the rendering of an environmental impact statement, efforts to manage these waters as a marine sanctuary were stalled. The governor of Hawaii withdrew state-controlled waters from the sanctuary proposal.

Although the National Marine Sanctuary Program was set up in 1972, its execution has been marred by politics, lack of funds, and bureaucratic delay. President Jimmy Carter ordered a speedup in the establishment of sanctuaries. But his efforts became entangled in a net of lobbies, protests, and pressures. At the same time as the Carter administration was calling for more marine sanctuaries, it was promoting oil and gas drilling on the outer continental shelf. The continental shelf is a kind of submarine platform that surrounds the continent. This shelf, or platform, extends outward from beaches, sloping into deep water and ending at a depth of 1,800 feet (5,400 m).

Environmentalists wanted no drilling for oil or gas in the outer continental shelf regions. Oil and gas interests joined together to eliminate the continental shelf regions as marine sanctuaries. However, the Carter administration did designate four marine sanctuaries. Two of them had restrictions against oil and gas drilling. When the Reagan administration came into office in 1980, it froze the oil and gas restrictions. But the administration later relented and reinstated the restrictions.

The designation of marine sanctuaries came to a halt during the eight years of the Reagan administration. Only one marine sanctuary was established during the term of the Reagan administration. However, the Reagan administration was not noted for its concern for the environment, either on land or in the sea.

EIGHT

A new form of whale exploitation—whale watching—has burgeoned over the past dozen years. Whale-watching fleets operate on the East and West coasts and ports in the Hawaiian Islands. This conservation-inspired activity draws thousands of people, young and old alike, to the coastal waters in the hope of seeing humpback, fin, minke, right, gray, and the rare blue and sperm whales.

EAST COAST
WHALE WATCHING

Whale-watching fleets on the East Coast operate from ports in Massachusetts and Maine. The most popular whale-watching port is located in Provincetown, Massachusetts, on the tip of Cape Cod. The oldest of the whale-watching fleets sailing from Provincetown is the Dolphin

WHALE WATCHERS CATCH A GLIMPSE OF
A RARE NORTH ATLANTIC RIGHT WHALE
OFF THE COAST OF NEW BRUNSWICK.

Fleet. This company originated whale watching on the East Coast. In its advertising, the Dolphin Fleet proclaims that "By sailing with us, you'll help save the whales." This fleet works closely with the Center for Coastal Studies, a Provincetown-based whale research group. Center scientists are on board Dolphin Fleet boats, guiding the search for whales and answering the questions of whale watchers.

A number of whale species may be seen off the Provincetown coast. These include the humpback, finback, right, and minke whales. Also seen in this region are the harbor porpoise, the Atlantic whitesided dolphin, the white-beaked dolphin, the killer whale, and the pilot whale.

The Center for Coastal Studies is the authority on the local populations of humpback whales. Center scientists have identified and named more than 250 humpback whales since 1975. Passengers on the Dolphin Fleet boats are provided with detailed histories of most of the humpbacks seen in the Provincetown waters. For the scientists, each whale-watching trip is a means of collecting more data on the endangered humpbacks. A popular pastime aboard the whale-watching boats is identifying individual humpback and right whales previously seen and coded. The behavior of the whales in the vicinity of the Dolphin boats is recorded by the scientists. Thus, passengers aboard a Dolphin Fleet boat are on not just a whale-watching voyage, but a scientific expedition.

Various environmental and scientific organizations use the Dolphin Fleet for their whale-observation activities. Included among them are the American Cetacean Society, the American Museum of Natural History, Greenpeace, the New Bedford Whaling Museum, the Audubon Society, and the Harvard Museum of Comparative Zoology.

Whale watching is somewhat like bird watching: One never knows what one will see, if anything. And, like bird watching, whale watching takes patience. The season runs from May to October off Provincetown. Despite the unpredictability of whale watching, hundreds of watchers are often treated to the aquatic antics of humpback whales with their breaching and fluke flapping. It might be said that Provincetown is the Mecca of eastern whale watchers.

WEST COAST
WHALE WATCHING

Whale watching on the West Coast is not quite the same as that on the New England coast. The gray whales do not behave in the same manner as the frolicking humpbacks. One advantage of West Coast whale watching is that gray whales may be seen from some land observation posts, such as on Point Reyes, California. Each fall, the gray whales start their southward migration from their summer habitat in the Bering Sea. The round-trip voyage of the gray whales is approximately 9,300 miles (15,000 km), the longest known migration route of any animal. The whales travel slowly, perhaps 5 to 7 kilometers (3.2 to 4.5 miles) an hour. They arrive off the California coast on their southern journey in December.

The gray whales continue their journey south, traveling about 620 miles (1,000 km) to the lagoons of Baja California in Mexico. These include Laguna San Ignacio, Puerto Adolfo Lopez Mateos, Scammon's Lagoon, and Bahia Magdalena. Several West Coast whale-watching fleets sail to these lagoons. They promise what they call "close encounters with whales." In Laguna San Ignacio, whale watchers try to take advantage of these promised encounters, rowing or paddling out to the gray whales and their calves in rowboats, canoes, kayaks, and rubber dinghies. Their hope is to come close enough to a whale

to touch it. One of the treats that Baja California whale watchers receive is a breaching of a gray whale. In this action, the whale leaps almost completely out of the water, then falls sideways or backward with a mighty splash.

IS WHALE WATCHING HARMFUL TO WHALES?

Because of the spectacular growth and popularity of whale watching, there is some concern among marine scientists that the activity may prove harmful to some species of whales. As more people become interested in the fascinating whales, more of them will go on whale-watching trips. This means a greater intrusion on the habitats and migration routes of the whales. A question arises: Will the whales be able to withstand or even coexist with the hordes of watchers and well-wishers that are expected in the decades ahead or will they be harmed by the invasion?

It is too early to tell. To prevent any conflict between whales and watchers on the East Coast, the National Marine Fisheries Service has set up rules and regulations aimed at protecting both whales and watchers. Whales must be treated with respect and caution because of their size. Most people have seen whales in movies or on television. They have no idea of the true size of these marvelous ocean mammals. The first sight of an adult sperm or finback whale can be an awesome experience.

WHALE WATCHERS IN CALIFORNIA CAN OBSERVE THE MIGRATION OF THE GRAY WHALES FROM THE BERING SEA TO THE LAGOONS OF BAJA CALIFORNIA.

It is illegal to harass or chase whales. People do this when trying to get close to a whale. The urge to touch an animal is strong. Human beings are contact animals; that is, we are accustomed to being touched from the moment of birth. Various animals are also contact animals—for example, the dog, cat, monkey, and rabbit. Some whales, particularly dolphins, do not seem to mind being touched. But since we do not know a great deal about the behavior of some whales, especially their reactions in the presence of boats and human beings, the best approach is one of caution.

Whale watchers sailing off the New England coast seem content to just watch the whales. Occasionally, some watchers in a small motorboat or other craft will try to get close to a whale. But there are strict rules that must be observed when sighting whales. Boats must stay at least 150 feet (45 m) from a whale. One never knows what a whale will do. Some may come up against the side of a boat; others may come up under it. Most whale-watching fleet captains are very experienced in maneuvering around whales and observe the rules.

When a whale-watching boat comes within the 150-foot range of a whale, the captain will idle the motor. This action reduces the possibility of injury to a whale by the rotating propellers. The idling motor serves another purpose. It lets the whale know the whereabouts of a boat. Whales rely on sounds to orient themselves. A silent boat could cause a collision between the boat and a submerged whale.

As outlined, whale watching is well regulated on the East Coast. This is because the National Marine Fisheries Service monitors the whale-watching activities. It is a different story in the lagoons of Baja California. These waters are under the jurisdiction of Mexico, a country not as conservation-oriented as the United States. Laxity in enforcing rules and regulations can mean harm to gray whales and to people. Gray whales breed and calve in the lagoons of Baja California. Mother whales can be very aggressive and protective when they have a calf at their side. Many mammals—wolves, bears, lions, and even the domestic dog and cat—resent human beings coming close to or touching their young. The ferocity and protectiveness of a black or grizzly bear when human beings come within sight of a bear family are well-known and documented. And so it can be with the gray whales. Although the adult whale may not object to being touched, it may object to anyone touching its calf. Even though the gray whales are baleen or toothless whales, they are powerful creatures. A flip of their flukes will smash a small boat, kayak, or canoe and send the occupants flying into the sea.

WHALE WATCHING AND WHALE MIGRATIONS

There is a concern that if some of the areas in the migratory routes of whales become congested with boats loaded with watchers, whales might change their routes. Is there any validity to this speculation? There is no indication, so far, that the East and West Coast whale travelers are planning on changing their centuries-old migratory routes because of the presence of human beings.

At the present time, there is little evidence to show that whale-watching activities are harmful to the whales. True, there have been some problems. For example, whales in the Baja California lagoons frolic very close to boats. They seem to be attracted by the hum of the boat motors. Some gray whales have actually taken still propellers into their mouths. Why do the gray whales come close to the boats? It is believed that the noise of slow-running boat motors is within the sound range of the gray whales. So far, there have been no major incidents involving whales, boats, or people.

IS WHALE
CONSERVATION WORKING?

Whale watching, the moratorium on commercial whaling, an awareness of the problems facing the whales, various research programs, whale sanctuaries, and the campaigns of environmental groups all have benefited the whales. Certainly, the whales have had a reprieve from persecution. But has this reprieve been in time for those species pushed close to the edge of extinction? Or have the heavily exploited species reached the point of no return? Only time will tell whether the depleted stocks of blue, finback, sei, sperm, humpback, gray, and right whales will bounce back to their former numbers.

We might say that whale conservation is working—to a degree. The major conservation measure for the harassed whales has been the moratorium. However, the moratorium is but a temporary halt in whaling. Indeed, the word itself means a period of permissive or obligatory delay. The moratorium on commercial whaling is subject to review. In a few years, the stocks of commercial whales will be reassessed. If stocks are deemed to be sufficient, an open season on whale hunting is to be expected. A number of nations will undoubtedly resume whaling operations when the International Whaling Commission gives the green light to commercial whaling activities.

In the meantime, whales must contend with oceanic pollution. The Arctic and Antarctic—the great feeding grounds of the great whales—are targeted for development. In 1988, more than thirty nations agreed to open up all of Antarctica to the development of oil and mineral resources. So far, this polar region has been kept free of any kind of major development. The proposed oil and mineral development could have a disastrous effect on the Antarctic's delicate ecosystems and could disturb the whale feeding grounds, according to environmentalists. A spokesperson for Greenpeace has stated that the pro-

WITH A FLOURISH, A SPERM WHALE SOUNDS.

posed Antarctic development has "done the Antarctic a great disservice." The United States is among the nations who have voted for the Antarctic development.

The California gray whales—a species that most certainly has benefited from conservation programs—may face a new threat in the years ahead. The U.S. Department of the Interior has plans to lease 1.1 million acres (.4 million ha) off the coast of northern California for oil and gas explorations. It will be recalled that gray whales travel through this region on their way to and from the Baja California lagoons.

And the conflict between Newfoundland fishermen and whales has not been resolved. Professor Jon Lien, the animal behaviorist at Memorial University in Newfoundland, is somewhat pessimistic about the impact of whale conservation on Newfoundland fisheries. He thinks whale conservation, in some instances, might have a boomerang effect, at least as far as whales and fishing nets are concerned.

As some whale populations increase—especially those of the humpback, fin, and right whales—so will the entanglement in fishing nets. The more whales coming into the Newfoundland fishery region, the more net accidents. Thus, Newfoundland fishermen are not enthusiastic about the efforts to save the whales and increase their populations.

• • •

There is no question that whale conservation reached a high level of success at the end of the 1980s. But environmentalists know the battle is not won. They know the importance of holding onto the gains made on behalf of the whales. Whether they can remains to be seen in the years left in the twentieth century. Politics and economics will undoubtedly play a major role in the future of the world's whales, as they have in the past.

SOURCES OF INFORMATION

American Littoral Society
Highlands, NJ 07732

Fisheries and Biological Services Directorate
Communications Director
Department of Fisheries and Oceans
200 Kent Street
Ottawa, Canada K1A 0E6

Information about whale-watching trips
off Provincetown, Massachusetts
(508) 487-3322

Greenpeace USA
1436 U Street N.W.
Washington, DC 20009

International Whaling Commission
The Red House
Station Road
Histon, Cambridge, England CB4 4NP

National Audubon Society
950 Third Avenue
New York, NY 10022

National Oceanic and Atmospheric Administration
Public Affairs
Herbert C. Hoover Building
14th and Constitution Avenue N.W.
Washington, DC 22030

National Wildlife Federation
1400 16th Street N.W.
Washington, DC 20036

Sierra Club
730 Polk Street
San Francisco, CA 94109

Whale Center
3929 Piedmont Avenue
Oakland, CA 94611

Whaling Museum
18 Johnny Cake Hill
New Bedford, MA 02740

Whale Protection Fund
1725 Desales Street, N.W.
Washington, DC 20036

BIBLIOGRAPHY

Books

Cousteau, Jacques-Yves. *The Whale: Mighty Monarch of the Sea.* New York: Doubleday, 1972.

Burns, Walter Noble. *A Year with a Whaler.* New York: Outing Publishing Company, 1913.

Leatherwood, Stephen, and Randall R. Reeves. *The Sierra Club Handbook of Whales and Dolphins.* San Francisco: Sierra Club Books, 1983.

Lien, Jon. *Wet and Fat: Whales and Seals of Newfoundland and Labrador.* St. John's, Newfoundland: Breakwater Books, 1985.

Magnolia, L. R. *Whales, Whaling and Whale Research: A Selective Bibliography.* New York: The Whaling Museum, Cold Spring Harbor, 1977.

Melville, Herman. *Moby Dick or the Whale.* New York: Modern Library, 1930.

Minasian, Stanley M., Kenneth Balcomb, and Larry Foster. *The World's Whales.* Washington, DC: Smithsonian Books, 1984.

Riedman, Sarah R., and Elton T. Gustafson. *Home Is the Sea for Whales.* New York: Rand McNally Company, 1966.

Robertson, R. B. *Of Whales and Men.* New York: Knopf, 1954.

Scheffer, Victor B. *The Year of the Whale*. New York: Scribner's Sons, 1969.

Small, George L. *The Blue Whale*. New York: Columbia University Press, 1972.

Zim, Herbert S. *The Great Whales*. New York: Scholastic Book Service, 1959.

Articles

"Caught in a Plastic Trap," *International Wildlife* (May–June 1986), pp. 22–23.

Center for Environmental Education. *U.S. Softens Stand on Research Whaling—Again*. Report No. 4 (February 1988).

Linden, Eugene. "Helping Out Putu, Siku, and Kanik," *Time* (October 31, 1988), pp. 76–77.

Martin, Marlene. "Encounter between Leviathans" [oil and bowhead whales], *Oceans* (September 1985), pp. 33–35.

McCloskey, Maxine. "Whaling by Any Other Name," *Oceans* (September 1985), pp. 65–66.

National television coverage of the rescue of the gray whales trapped in the icepack off Point Barrow, Alaska, October 18 through 28, 1988.

National Oceanic and Atmospheric Administration, Annual Report for 1987–88. U.S. Department of Commerce, Washington, D.C.

"Whales Flock to the Tourists," *New Scientist* (October 1984).

New York Times articles:

"Advertisement: The Dolphin Massacre off Our Coast: What You Can Do to Stop It" (April 11, 1988), sec. D, p. 11.

"Pollution Is Blamed in Whale Deaths" (January 12, 1988), sec. C, p. 7.

"Senate Panel Urged to Toughen Curbs on Killing of Dolphins" (April 14, 1988), sec. A, p. 31.

"Sludge Dumping at Sea: No End in Sight" (February 28, 1988), sec. II, p. 1.

"Tainted Fish Found in Dead Whales on Cape Cod" (December 20, 1987), p. 28.

"U.S. Denies Japan Plea on Fishing" (April 7, 1988), sec. A, p. 1.

"U.S. Warns Japan Not to Kill Whales in Antarctic" (January 22, 1988), sec. A, p. 7.

United Nations. *Report on the Conference of the Human Environment*, Stockholm and New York, 1973.

INDEX

31969
31969

639.9   McCoy, J. J.
MCC
         The plight of the
         whales

$12.90

DATE			
OCT 9 '90			
OCT 9 '90			
MR 15 '91			
JAN 22 1993			
MR 31 '95			
MAR 2 2 1999